A Collection of the
Proverbs of All Nations

Compared, Explained, and Illustrated

Walter K. Kelly

Edited by

Wolfgang Mieder

"Proverbium"
in cooperation with the
Department of German and Russian

The University of Vermont
Burlington, Vermont
2002

Supplement Series

of

Proverbium
Yearbook of International Proverb Scholarship

Edited by Wolfgang Mieder

Volume 11

Cover illustration taken from Wolfgang Mieder's
private copy of Walter K. Kelly,
A Collection of the Proverbs of All Nations.
Andover, Massachusetts: Warren F. Draper, 1869.

ISBN 0-9710223-5-6

PN
6405
.K5
2002

Manufactured in the United States of America
by Queen City Printers Inc.
Burlington, Vermont

INTRODUCTION

One would not think that someone who has written and translated numerous books would be as obscure a person as Walter Keating Kelly. Despite the expert help of my library colleagues Jake Barickman, Patricia Mardeusz, and Nancy Rosedale at the University of Vermont and the attempts by fellow folklorist Fionnuala Williams from the Institute of Irish Studies at the Queen's University of Belfast, very little information could be obtained on this scholar and translator. Our joint efforts resulted in the following scant portray of Walter Kelly who in addition to other volumes happens to have authored *A Collection of the Proverbs of All Nations* (1859).

As far as I could ascertain, Walter K. Kelly was born in 1806 at Dublin, Ireland. In 1822 he entered Trinity College in his hometown, obtaining his Bachelor of Arts degree in 1827. He seems to have worked for the publishing house of Henry G. Bohn at London, and it might well be that Bohn's own proverb collection *A Polyglot of Foreign Proverbs, Comprising French, Italian, German, Dutch, Spanish, Portuguese, and Danish, with English Translations* (1857) inspired him to write his own book. Bohn had also published *A Hand-Book of Proverbs Comprising an Entire Republication of Ray's Collection of English Proverbs, with Additions from Foreign Languages* (1855), thus in fact presenting Kelly with two invaluable sources for his annotated volume.[1]

Certainly Kelly kept busy writing such books as *Syria and the Holy Land* (1844), *Narrative of the French Revolution of 1848* (1848), *History of the Year 1848* (1849), *The Life of Wellington* (1853), and *The History of Russia*, 2 vols. (1855). As an historian, he also translated various works from the French and German into English, notably Jean-Henri Merle d'Aubigné's *History of the Reformation* (1842), Leopold Ranke's *The Ottoman and the Spanish Empires* (1843), and many others.[2] But Kelly was also the author of various poems and provided literal translations of Latin and French literature for "Bohn's Library" books.[3] In addition, he must have been quite active as the author of essays and reviews on literary and historical topics,

---

[1]Both volumes have been reprinted; the first in 1968 by the Gale Research Company in Detroit, Michigan, the second also in 1968 by the AMS Press in New York, New York.

[2]See the short entries under "Walter Keating Kelly" in S. Austin Allibone, *A Critical Dictionary of English Literature and British and American Authors*, 2 vols. (Philadelphia: J.B. Lippincott, 1871), vol. 1, p. 1014; and John Foster Kirk, *A Supplement to Allibone's Critical Dictionary of English Literature and British and American Authors* (Philadelphia: J.B. Lippincott, 1891), p. 936.

[3]See the four-line note on "Walter Keating Kelly" in D.J. O'Donoghue, *The Poets of Ireland. A Biographical and Bibliographical Dictionary of Irish Writers of English Verse* (Dublin: Hodges Figgis, 1912), p. 228.

publishing his insights in such prestigious journals as the *London Quarterly Review* and the *Westminster Review*. In fact, he was the editor of the *Foreign Quarterly Review* from 1844 to 1846.[4] When he died in 1873, most likely at Dublin, he had amassed a considerable volume of writings and translations. Some literary historian would do well to study Kelly's life and works, since he obviously was a significant force during the nineteenth century.

There is yet one other book to be mentioned that shows that Walter Kelly had some definite interest in folklore, of which proverbs are, of course, a small part. This is his volume on *Curiosities of Indo-European Tradition and Folk-Lore* (1863) that is above all a treatise on mythology, dealing primarily with the works of such German scholars as Jacob Grimm and Adalbert Kuhn. Some of the chapters deal with the common origin of the mythologies of the Indo-European nations, treating such matters as the descent of fire, the dead, the gods, the wild hunt, etc. As Kelly states in his preface, "the purpose of this book is to make known some of the most remarkable discoveries which have been achieved by the successors and countrymen of Jacob Grimm, and to indicate, in a manner not too abstruse for the general reader, the method and line of research which they have pursued, with a success in

---

[4]See the incomplete information in Walter E. Houghton (ed.), *The Wellesley Index to Victorian Periodicals, 1824-1900*, 5 vols. (Toronto: University of Toronto Press, 1966-1989), vol. 2, p. 969; and vol. 5, p. 425.

some instances surpassing all expectations."[5] Writing and translating for "the general reader" was Kelly's major purpose in his endeavors, and since he was clearly a polyglot, he approached his various subject matters from a valuable comparative point of view. This intercultural approach also informs his book entitled *A Collection of the Proverbs of All Nations. Compared, Explained, and Illustrated*. Its first edition appeared in 1859 with W. Kent & Co. at London. The same publisher brought out a second edition in 1861 and a third in 1870. In 1877 the book appeared once more in London with Diprose & Bateman in "Diprose's Railway Library" meant for general readers. However, Kelly's readable and informative treasure trove of proverbs from many languages and cultures also made the jump across the ocean to the American market. It was published by Warren F. Draper in 1869 at Andover, Massachusetts,[6] with a second identical printing in 1879. The latter has been reprinted three times: Folcroft Library Editions of Darby, Pennsylvania, reissued a limited edition of 150 copies in 1972; Norwood Editions of Norwood, Pennsylvania, reprinted a mere 100 copies in 1977; and R. West of Philadelphia must have brought out a minute number of

---

[5]Walter K. Kelly, *Curiosities of Indo-European Tradition and Folk-Lore* (London: Chapman & Hall, 1863; rpt. Detroit, Michigan: Singing Tree Press, 1969), p. v.

[6]This first American edition of 1869 from my proverb archive serves as the original for this reprint.

volumes in 1978, since only two copies could be located in North America.

With the various 19th-century editions and three extant reprints one would think that a new reprint would be like carrying coals to Newcastle, to put it proverbially. And yet, nothing could be further from the truth. In a letter of 22 April 2003, my Irish friend Fionnuala Williams reported to me that she could not locate Kelly's *A Collection of the Proverbs of All Nations* in any libraries of his native Ireland, nor had she as a well-known paremiologist ever come across it. An extensive library search by my colleague Nancy Rosedale located a mere 93 copies in British and North American libraries. Obviously the 250 plus reprints must not have sold very well, and the 19th-century editions might also have been rather small and somehow did not get into many major libraries. And yet, Kelly would doubtlessly have been pleased to learn that his small volume made it into the private paremiographical libraries and/or bibliographies of such great proverb scholars as Giuseppe Pitrè (Italy), Ignace Bernstein (Poland), Thomas Arthur Stephens (England), and Otto Moll (Germany).[7] The volume, meant

[7]Giuseppe Pitrè, *Bibliografia delle tradizioni popolari d'Italia* (Palermo: Carlo Clausen, 1894), p. 217 (nos. 2911-2913); Ignace Bernstein, *Catalogue des livres parémiologiques composant la bibliothèque de Ignace Bernstein*, 2 vols. (Varsovie: W. Drugulin, 1900; reprint ed. by Wolfgang Mieder. Hildesheim: Georg Olms, 2003), vol. 1, p. 407 (no. 1684); Wilfrid Bonser, *Proverb Literature. A Bibliography of Works Relating to Proverbs, Compiled from Materials Left by the Late T.A. Stephens*

for the general market, might simply have found its way primarily into private hands or small-town lending libraries that are not necessarily attached to electronic networks. There is then plenty of justification in making Walter Kelly's intriguing and informative polyglot proverb collection with its enlightening and entertaining explanations and annotations available once again.

Turning now to Walter K. Kelly's unpretentious volume of merely 232 pages, it is obvious at once that its author could not possibly have done justice to the somewhat overinclusive title of *A Collection of the Proverbs of all Nations*. In fact, in his two-page preface Kelly is much more modest, stating clearly at the outset that his annotated proverb collection is meant for "general use" (v), i.e., he lays no claim to an extensive or even inclusive treatment of English proverbs and their equivalents or parallels from many different nations. He had studied Richard Chenevix Trench's slim but important volume on *Proverbs and Their Lessons* (1853) carefully,[8] wishing to fulfill Trench's call for a general proverb collection that goes

---

(London: William Glaisher, 1930; rpt. Nendeln/Liechtenstein: Kraus Reprint, 1967), p. 13 (no. 97); and Otto Moll, *Sprichwörterbibliographie* (Frankfurt am Main: Vittorio Klostermann, 1958), p. 31 (no. 385).

[8]See Richard Chenevix Trench, *Proverbs and Their Lessons* (London: George Routledge, 1905; reprint ed. by Wolfgang Mieder. Burlington, Vermont: The University of Vermont, 2003), pp. vii-viii.

beyond just listing texts but rather also includes valuable explanatory comments with references to equal or similar proverbs in other languages. Wanting to make this a book to read rather than just a list of proverbs,[9] Kelly started with a set of basic English proverbs, added foreign texts to them in English translation with their original texts appearing as notes on the bottom of the pages,[10] and then grouped his rich textual materials with his readable comments into forty-four small chapters. The long table of "Contents" shows at a glance that there are such topics as "Women, Love, Marriage", "Friendship", "Luck, Fortune, Misfortune", "Industry and Idleness", "Moderation, Excess", "Experience", "Truth, Falsehood, Honesty", "Speech, Silence", "Wealth, Poverty, Plenty, Want", "Law and Lawyers", "Clergy", "National and Local Characteristics, Local Allusions", and many more. The book's usefulness would be quite limited for the scholar, had

---

[9]For a short description of Walter Kelly's book see the review essay (without author or title) of 19 books on proverbs in *The Quarterly Review*, 125 (1868), 217-254 (here pp. 249-250). The reviewer begins with this complimentary statement: "Unowned [i.e., anonymous] proverbs are often most characteristic and noticeable. Of these a rare modern collection has been made by Mr. W.K. Kelly, much to be recommended to such as would study the subject coherently and continuously" (p. 249).

[10]Kelly might have received this idea from Trench's book who includes many foreign proverbs in English translation in his prose, supplying their original wording in the footnotes. There can be no doubt that Trench had a considerable influence on Kelly's methodology.

Kelly not also included an extensive "Index" (223-232) of the English key-words of the proverbs that makes the location of every text possible.

As has been mentioned, the scope of Kelly's book is not quite as global as its title would suggest. But there are certainly texts from such varied languages and cultures as American, Arabic, Basque, Chinese, Dutch, English, French, German, Greek, Hebrew, Irish, Italian, Persian. Polish, Portuguese, Russian, Scottish, Spanish, Welsh, and others. Nevertheless, most of the texts stem from European languages, and Walter Kelly's claim of presenting "proverbs of all nations" is somewhat exaggerated. This is also true to some degree regarding the explanations of the proverbs. Quite often Kelly presents merely the texts without any comments, but then there are also numerous comments about the origin, history, and meaning of certain proverbs that are true gems, varying in length from a solid paragraph to two whole pages. This is true, for example, for the proverbs "The collier (or charcoal burner) is master in his own house" (35-36), "One beats the bush and another catches the birds" (45-46), "Don't buy a pig in a poke" (58), "For a point Martin lost his ass" (84-85), "As the fool thinks, the bell tinks" (88-89), "You may pay too dear for your whistle" (91-92; with reference to Benjamin Franklin), "To build castles in the air" (138-139; actually a proverbial expression), "There's many a slip 'twixt the cup and the lip" (140-141), "Many ways to kill a dog besides hanging him" (152-153), "It is well said, but who will bell the cat" (170-171), "Murder will out" (174-175), etc. As Kelly relates various etiological tales explaining the supposed origin of a proverb, he cautions readers that its actual beginning is quite different, the account being but "one of a thousand instances in which a story growing out of a proverb has been presented as that proverb's origin" (116).[11]

In any case, Kelly delights in presenting such folk etymological tales and then setting forth the truth of the matter. This is exactly what makes this volume so entertaining for the general reader. Its readability is also enhanced by some of Kelly's personal comments, as for example at the beginning of his discussion of the well-known proverb about outside appearances: "*Beauty is but skin deep*. The saying itself is no deeper. It is physically untrue, for beauty is not an accident of surface, but a natural result and attribute of a fine organization [...]" (7-8). There is also the American proverb "Let every man skin his own skunk" with the explanation that "the skunk stinks ten thousand times worse than a polecat" (102). And for a bit of humor, Kelly also includes some wellerisms like "'What a dust do I raise!' said the fly, as it sat upon the axle of the

---

[11]See Archer Taylor, *The Proverb* (Cambridge, Massachusetts: Harvard University Press, 1931; rpt. Hatboro, Pennsylvania: Folklore Associates, 1962; reprint again with an introduction and bibliography by Wolfgang Mieder. Bern: Peter Lang, 1985), pp. 27-32. See also Pack Carnes (ed.), *Proverbia in Fabula. Essays on the Relationship of the Fable and the Proverb* (Bern: Peter Lang, 1988).

chariot" (98; see also 107-108).[12] The final chapter
on "National and Local Characteristics" (212-222) is of
special interest as well since it touches on the problem
of stereotypical proverbs.[13]

Let me stop here, since Kelly's book is best appreci-
ated by simply opening its pages anywhere and enjoy-
ing the numerous proverbs from many lands. Again,
this is not a particularly scholarly volume, but it
certainly fulfills its purpose of providing general
readers with an entertaining introduction to the similar-
ities and differences of the proverbial wisdom among
the people of the world. As expected, there are by now
many more complete and erudite international proverb
collections on the book market, as can be seen from
the following select bibliography. Whoever needs more
detailed and precise information, should turn to these
volumes, but those readers who wish to spend a few
pleasant hours perusing the truly fascinating world of
proverbs will certainly be very well served by Walter
Keating Kelly's still enjoyable *Collection of the Proverbs of All Nations*. This reprint then is intended to
make this valuable experience possible for modern
readers who will find many proverbs in the book to reflect and descant upon.

---

[12]See Wolfgang Mieder and Stewart A. Kingsbury, *A
Dictionary of Wellerisms* (New York: Oxford University Press,
1994), p. 37.

[13]See Abraham A. Roback, *A Dictionary of International
Slurs* (Cambridge, Massachusetts: Sci-Art Publishers, 1944; rpt.
Waukesha, Wisconsin: Maledicta Press, 1979).

International Proverb Collections

Bilgrav, Jens Aage Stabell. *20,000 Proverbs and Their Equivalents in German, French, Swedish, Danish.* Copenhagen: Hans Heide, 1985.

Bohn, Henry G. *A Polyglot of Foreign Proverbs, Comprising French, Italian, German, Dutch, Spanish, Portuguese, and Danish, with English Translations and a General Index.* London: Henry G. Bohn, 1857; rpt. Detroit, Michigan: Gale Research Company, 1968.

Champion, Selwyn Gurney. *Racial Proverbs. A Selection of the World's Proverbs Arranged Linguistically with Authoritative Introductions to the Proverbs of 27 Countries and Races.* London: George Routledge, 1938; rpt. London: Routledge & Kegan, 1963.

Christy, Robert. *Proverbs, Maxims and Phrases of All Ages.* New York: G.P. Putnam's Sons, 1887; rpt. Norwood, Pennsylvania: Norwood Editions, 1977.

Cordry, Harold V. *The Multicultural Dictionary of Proverbs.* Jefferson, North Carolina: McFarland, 1997.

Davidoff, Henry. *A World Treasury of Proverbs from Twenty-Five Languages.* New York: Random House, 1946.

Fergusson, Rosalind. *The Facts on File Dictionary of Proverbs.* New York: Facts on File, 1983.

xii   Introduction

Flonta, Teodor. *A Dictionary of English and Romance Languages Equivalent Proverbs*. Hobart, Tasmania: DeProverbio.com, 2001.

Glusky, Jerzy. *Proverbs. A Comparative Book of English, French, German, Italian, Spanish and Russian Proverbs with a Latin Appendix*. New York: Elsevier Publishing, 1971.

Iscla, Luis. *English Proverbs and Their Near Equivalents in Spanish, French, Italian and Latin*. New York: Peter Lang, 1995.

Kuusi, Matti. *Proverbia septentrionalia. 900 Balto-Finnic Proverb Types with Russian, Baltic, German and Scandinavian Parallels*. Helsinki: Suomalainen Tiedeakatemia, 1985.

Lawson, J. Gilchrist. *The World's Best Proverbs and Maxims*. New York: Grosset & Dunlap, 1926.

Ley, Gerd de. *International Dictionary of Proverbs*. New York: Hippocrene Books, 1998.

Mawr, E.B. *Analogous Proverbs in Ten Languages*. London: Elliot Stock, 1885.

Middlemore, James. *Proverbs, Sayings and Comparisons in Various Languages*. London: Isbister, 1889.

Mieder, Wolfgang. *The Prentice-Hall Encyclopedia of World Proverbs*. Englewood Cliffs, New Jersey: Prentice-Hall, 1986.

Paczolay, Gyula. *European Proverbs in 55 Languages with Equivalents in Arabic, Persian, Sanskrit, Chinese and Japanese*. Veszprém: Veszprémi Nyomda, 1997.

Stevenson, Burton. *The Home Book of Proverbs, Maxims and Familiar Phrases*. New York: Macmillan, 1948.

Strauss, Emanuel. *Dictionary of European Proverbs*. 3 vols. London: Routledge, 1994.

Strauss, Emanuel. *Concise Dictionary of European Proverbs*. London: Routledge, 1998.

Yoo, Young H. *Wisdom of the Far East. A Dictionary of Proverbs, Maxims, and Famous Classical Phrases of the Chinese, Japanese, and Korean*. Washington, D.C.: Far Eastern Research and Publications Center, 1972.

Yurtbasi, Metin. *Turkish Proverbs and Their Equivalents in Fifteen Languages*. Istanbul: Serkon Etiket, 1996.

Burlington, Vermont
Winter 2002

Wolfgang Mieder

A COLLECTION

OF THE

PROVERBS OF ALL NATIONS.

𝔠ompared, 𝔈xplained, and 𝔍llustrated,

BY

WALTER K. KELLY.

ANDOVER:

WARREN F. DRAPER,

MAIN STREET.

1869.

" Even the best proverb, though often the expression of the widest experience in the choicest language, can be thoroughly misapplied. It can not embrace the whole of the subject, and apply in all cases like a mathematical formula. Its wisdom lies in the ear of the hearer." — FRIENDS IN COUNCIL.

PREFACE.

—◆—

Enɢʟɪsʜ literature, in most departments the richest in Europe, is yet the only one in which there has hitherto existed no comprehensive collection of proverbs adapted to general use. To supply this deficiency is the object of the present attempt.

Dean Trench, in the preface to his "Proverbs and their Lessons," adverts to "the immense number and variety of books bearing on the subject;" but adds, that among them all he knows not one which appears to him quite suitable for all readers. "Either," he says, "they include matter which cannot fitly be placed before all — or they address themselves to the scholar alone; or, if not so, are at any rate inaccessible to the mere English reader — or they contain bare lists of proverbs, with no endeavor to compare, illustrate, or explain them — or, if they do seek to explain, they yet do it without attempting to sound the depths or measure the real significance of that which they attempt to unfold."

My own experience in this department of literature is entirely in accordance with these views. I have, therefore, during the preparation of the following pages, kept constantly before my mind the Dean of Westminster's precise statement of things to be done, and things to be avoided.

British proverbs, for the most part, form the basis of this collection. They are arranged according to their import and affinity,

and under each of them are grouped translations of their principal
equivalents in other languages, the originals being generally ap-
pended in footnotes. By this means are formed natural families
of proverbs, the several members of which acquire increased significance from the light they reflect on each other. At the same
time, a source of lively interest is opened for the reader, who is
thus enabled to observe the manifold diversities of form which the
same thought assumes, as expressed in different times and by
many distinct races of men; to trace the unity in variety which
pervades the oldest and most universal monuments of opinion and
sentiment among mankind; and to verify for himself the truth
of Lord Bacon's well-known remark, that " the genius, wit, and
spirit of a nation are discovered in its proverbs."

Touching as they do upon so wide a range of human concerns,
proverbs are necessarily associated with written literature. Sometimes they are created by it; much oftener they are woven into its
texture. Personal anecdotes turn upon them in many instances;
and not unfrequently they have figured in national history, or have
helped to preserve the memory of events, manners, usages, and
ideas, some of which have left little other record of their existence.
From the wealth of illustration thus inviting my hand, I have
sought to gather whatever might elucidate and enliven my subject
without overlaying it. In this way I hope to have overcome the
general objection alleged by Isaac Disraeli against collections of
proverbs, on the ground of their " unreadableness." It is true, as
he says, that " taking in succession a multitude of insulated proverbs, their slippery nature resists all hope of retaining one in a
hundred; " but this remark, I venture to believe, does not apply
to the present collection, in which proverbs are not insulated, but
presented in orderly, coherent groups, and accompanied with
appropriate accessories, so as to fit them for being considered with
some continuity of thought.

CONTENTS.

PROVERBS OF ALL NATIONS.

WOMEN, LOVE, MARRIAGE, ETC.

What's sauce for the goose is sauce for the gander.

THIS is an Englishwoman's proverb. The Italian
sisterhood complain that " In men every mortal sin is
venial; in women every venial sin is mortal."[1] These
are almost the only proverbs relating to women in which
justice is done to them, all the rest being manifestly the
work of the unfair sex.

> **If a woman were as little as she is good,**
> **A peascod would make her a gown and a hood.**

This is Ray's version of an Italian slander.[2] The
Germans say, " Every woman would rather be handsome than good;"[3] and that, indeed, " There are only
two good women in the world: one of them is dead,

---

[1] A gli uomini ogni peccato mortale è veniale, alle donne ogni
veniale è mortale.

[2] Se la donna fosse piccola come è buona, la minima foglia la
farebbe una veste e una corona.

[3] Jedes Weib will lieber schön als fromm sein.

and the other is not to be found."[1] The French, in spite of their pretended gallantry, have the coarseness to declare that "A man of straw is worth a woman of gold;"[2] and even the Spaniard, who sometimes speaks words of stately courtesy towards the female sex, advises you to "Beware of a bad woman, and put no trust in a good one."[3]

> " The crab of the wood is sauce very good
> For the crab of the sea;
> But the wood of the crab is sauce for a drab,
> That will not her husband obey."

A spaniel, a woman, and a walnut tree,
The more they 're beaten the better they be.

There is Latin authority for this barbarous distich.[4] The Italians say, "Women, asses, and nuts require rough hands."[5] Much wiser is the Scotch adage, —

Ye may ding the deil into a wife, but ye'll ne'er ding him out o' her.

Take your wife's first advice, and not her second.

The French make the rule more general — "Take a woman's first advice, etc."[6] There is good reason for this if the Italian proverb is true, "Women are wise

---

[1] Es giebt nur zwei gute Weiber auf der Welt: die Eine ist gestorben, die Andere nicht zu finden.

[2] Un homme de paille vaut une femme d'or.

[3] De la mala muger te guarda, y de la buena no fies nada.

[4] Nux, asinus, mulier simili sunt lege ligata,
Hæc tria nil recte faciunt si verbera cessant.

[5] Donne, asini, e noci voglion le mani atroci.

[6] Prends le premier conseil d'une femme, et non le second.

offhand, and fools on reflection."[1] They have less logical minds than men, but surpass them in quickness of intuition, having, says Dean Trench, "what Montaigne ascribes to them in a remarkable word, *l'esprit prime-sautier* — the leopard's spring, which takes its prey, if it be to take it at all, at the first bound." "Summer-sown corn and women's advice turn out well once in seven years,"[2] say the Germans; and the Spaniards hold that "A woman's counsel is no great thing, but he who does not take it is a fool."[3] In Servia they say, "It is sometimes right even to obey a sensible wife;" and they tell this story in elucidation of the proverb. A Herzegovinian once asked a Kadi whether a man ought to obey his wife, whereupon the Kadi answered that he needed not to do so. The Herzegovinian then continued: "My wife pressed me this morning to bring thee a pot of beef suet, so I have done well in not obeying her." Then said the Kadi, "Verily, it is sometimes right even to obey a sensible wife."

It's nae mair ferlie to see a woman greet than to see a guse gang
barefit. — *Scotch.*

That is, it is no more wonder to see a woman cry than to see a goose go barefoot. "Women laugh when they can, and weep when they will."[4] This is a French proverb, translated by Ray. Its want of rhyme makes it probable that it was never naturalized in England.

---

1 La donna savia è all' impensata, alla pensata è matta.
2 Sommersaat und Weiberrath geräth alle sieben Jahre einmal.
3 El consejo de la muger es poco, y quien no le toma es loco.
4 Femme rit quand elle peut, et pleure quand elle veut.

The Italians say, " A woman complains, a woman's in woe, a woman is sick, when she likes to be so,"[1] and that " A woman's tears are a fountain of craft."[2]

A woman's mind and winter wind change oft.

" Women are variable as April weather" (German).[3] " Women, wind, and fortune soon change" (Spanish).[4] Francis I. of France wrote one day with a diamond on a window of the château of Chambord, —

" Souvent femme varie :
Bien fou qui s'y fie."

" A woman changes oft :
Who trusts her is right soft."

His sister, Queen Margaret of Navarre, entered the room as he was writing the ungallant couplet, and, protesting against such a slander on her sex, she declared that she could quote twenty instances of man's fickleness. Francis retorted that her reply was not to the point, and that he would rather hear one instance of woman's constancy. " Can you mention a single instance of her inconstancy?" asked the Queen of Navarre. It happened that a few weeks before this conversation a gentleman of the court had been thrown into prison upon a serious charge; and his wife, who was one of the queen's ladies in waiting, was reported

---

[1] Donna si lagna, donna si duole, donna s'ammala quando la vuole.

[2] Lagrime di donna, fontana di malizia.

[3] Weiber sind veränderlich wie Aprilwetter.

[4] Muger, viento, y ventura presto se muda.

to have eloped with his page. Certain it was that the page and the lady had fled, no one could tell whither. Francis triumphantly cited this case; but Margaret warmly defended the lady, and said that time would prove her innocence. The king shook his head, but promised that if, within a month, her character should be reëstablished, he would break the pane on which the couplet was written, and grant his sister whatever boon she might ask. Many days had not elapsed after this, when it was discovered that it was not the lady who had fled with the page, but her husband. During one of her visits to him in prison they had exchanged clothes, and he was thus enabled to deceive the jailer, and effect his escape, while the devoted wife remained in his place. Margaret claimed his pardon at the king's hand, who not only granted it, but gave a grand fête and tournament to celebrate this instance of conjugal affection. He also destroyed the pane of glass, but the calumnious saying inscribed on it has unfortunately survived.

> A woman's tongue wags like a lamb's tail.
>
> A woman's strength is in her tongue. — *Welsh.*
>
> Arthur could not tame a woman's tongue. — *Welsh.*

"Three women and three geese make a market,"[1] according to the Italians. "Foxes are all tail, and women are all tongue;" at least, it is so in Auvergne.[2] "All women are good Lutherans," say the Danes;

---

[1] Tre oche e tre donne fann' un mercato.

[2] Les femmes sont faites de langue, comme les renards de queue.

"they would rather preach than hear mass."[1] "A woman's tongue is her sword, and she does not let it rust," is a saying of the Chinese.

Swine, women, and bees are not to be turned.

"Because" is a woman's answer.

And not so unmeaning an answer as flippant critics imagine. It is an example of that much-admired figure of speech, aposiopesis, and means — because I will have it so. "What a woman wills, God wills" (French).[2] "Whatever a woman will she can" (Italian).[3]

> "The man's a fool who thinks by force or skill
> To stem the torrent of a woman's will ;
> For if she will, she will, you may depend on 't,
> And if she won't, she won't, and there's an end on 't"

The cunning of the sex is equal to their obstinacy. "Women know a point more than the devil" (Italian).[4] What wonder, then, if "A bag of fleas is easier to keep guard over than a woman"? (German)[5] The wilfulness of woman is pleasantly hinted at in the Scotch proverb, "'Gie her her will, or she'll burst,' quoth the gudeman when his wife was dinging him."

A woman conceals what she does not know.

Women and bairns lein [conceal] what they kenna. — *Scotch.*

"To a woman and a magpie tell what you would

---

[1] Alle Quinder ere gode Lutherske, de predike heller end de höre Messe.

[2] Ce que femme veut, Dieu le veut.

[3] Se la donna vuol, tutto la puol.

[4] Le donne sanno un punto più del diavolo.

[5] Ein Sack voll Flöhe ist leichter zu hüten wie ein Weib.

speak in the market-place" (Spanish).[1] Hotspur says
to his wife, —

> " Constant you are,
> But yet a woman, and for secrecy
> No lady closer; for I well believe
> Thou wilt not utter what thou dost not know,
> And so far I will trust thee, gentle Kate."

But, if there is truth in proverbs, men have no right to
reproach women for blabbing. A woman can at least
keep her own secret. Try her on the subject of her
age.

Beauty draws more than oxen.

" One hair of a woman draws more than a bell-rope "
German).[2]

> " And beauty draws us with a single hair."

Beauty buys no beef.
Beauty is no inheritance.

In spite of these curmudgeon maxims, let no fair
maid despair whose face is her fortune, for " She that is
born a beauty is born married" (Italian).[3]

Beauty is but skin deep.

The saying itself is no deeper. It is physically untrue, for beauty is not an accident of surface, but a natural result and attribute of a fine organization. A man
may sneer, like Ralph Nickleby, at a lovely face, be-

---

[1] A la muger y a la picaza loque dirias en la plaza.
[2] Ein Frauenhaar zieht mehr als ein Glockenseil.
[3] Chi nasce bella, nasce maritata.

cause he chooses rather to see "the grinning death's head beneath it;" but Ralph was a heartless villain, and that is only another name for a fool. " Beauty is one of God's gifts," says Mr. Lewes, "and every one really submits to its influence, whatever platitudes he may think needful to issue. . . . . . How, think you, should we ever have relished the immortal fragments of Greek literature, if our conception of Greek men and Greek women had been formed by the contemplation of figures such as those of Chinese art? Would any pulse have throbbed at the Labdacidan tale had the descendants of Labdacus risen before the imagination with obese rotundity, large ears, gashes of mouths, eyes lurching upwards towards the temples, and no nose to speak of? Could we with any sublime emotions picture to ourselves Fo-Ti on the Promethean rock, or a Congou Antigone wailing her unwedded death?"

Fine feathers make fine fowls.

Therefore, "If you want a wife, choose her on Saturday, not on Sunday" (Spanish);[1] *i. e.*, choose her in undress. "No woman is ugly when she is dressed" (Spanish);[2] at least, she is not so in her own opinion. "The swarthy dame, dressed fine, decries the fair one" (Spanish).[3]

The fairer the hostess the fouler the reckoning.

"A handsome landlady is bad for the purse" (French);[4]

---

[1] Si quieres hembra, escoge la el sabado, y no el domingo.
[2] Compuesta no hay muger fea.
[3] Baza compuesta la blanca denuesta.
[4] Belle hôtesse, c'est un mal pour la bourse.

for this among other reasons — that "If the landlady is fair, the wine too is fair" (German).[1]

A bonny bride is sune buskit. — *Scotch.*

Buskit — dressed. She needs little adornment to enhance her charms.

Joan is as good as my lady in the dark.
When candles are all out cats are gray.

"Blemishes are unseen by night,"[2] says an ancient Latin proverb; and the Greeks held that "When the lamp is removed all women are alike."[3] Opinions may differ on that point, but all agree that

"The night
Shows stars and women in a better light."

Hence the Italian warning, to choose "Neither jewel, nor woman, nor linen by candlelight;"[4] and the French hyperbole, "By candlelight a goat looks a lady."[5]

If Jack is in love he is no judge of Jill's beauty.

"Nobody's sweetheart is ugly" (Dutch).[6] "Never seemed a prison fair or a mistress foul" (French).[7] "Handsome is not what is handsome, but what pleases" (Italian).[8] "He whose fair one squints says she ogles"

---

[1] Ist die Wirthin schön, ist auch der Wein schön.
[2] Nocte latent mendæ.
[3] Λυχνοῦ ἀρθέντος πᾶσα γυνὴ ἡ αὐτή.
[4] Ne gioia, ne donna, ne tela al lume de candela.
[5] A la chandelle la chèvre semble demoiselle.
[6] Niemands lief is lelijk.
[7] Il n'est point de belles prisons ni de laides amours.
[8] Non è bello quel che è bello, ma quel che piace.

(German).[1] "'Red is Love's color,' said the wooer to his foxy charmer" (German).[2]

Love is blind.

Blind to all imperfections in the beloved object; blind also to everything around it — to facts, consequences, and prudential considerations. "People in love think that other people's eyes are out" (Spanish).[3]

It is hard to keep flax from the lowe [fire]. — *Scotch.*

"Man is fire, woman tow, and the devil comes and blows" (Spanish).[4]

Glasses and lasses are bruckle [brittle] wares. — *Scotch.*

A pretty girl and a tattered gown are sure to find some hook in the way.

Italy appears to be the original country of this proverb, though it is popularly current in Ulster. "A handsome woman and a pinked or slashed garment" are the things mentioned in the Italian proverb.[5] The French form [6] corresponds with the Irish.

Where love fails we espy all faults.

Faults are thick where love is thin. — *Welsh.*

---

[1] Wessen Huldin schielt, der sagt sie liebaugele.

[2] "Roth ist die Farbe der Liebe," sagte der Buhler zu seinem fuchs farbenen Schatz.

[3] Piensan los enamorados que tienen los otros los ojos quebrados.

[4] El hombre es el fuego, la muger la estopa; viene el diablo y sopla.

[5] Bella donna e veste tagliazzata sempre s'imbatte in qualche uncino.

[6] Belle fille et méchante robe trouvent toujours qui les accroche.

Hot love is soon cold.

Love me little, love me long.

Love of lads and fire of chats are soon in and soon out. — *Derbyshire.*

Chats, *i. e.,* chips.

Lads' love's a busk of broom, hot a while and soon done. — *Cheshire.*

Love is never without jealousy.

"He that is not jealous is not in love," says St. Augustin;[1] but that depends not only upon the disposition of the lover, but upon the point arrived at in the history of his love. Doubts and fears are excusable in one who has not yet had assurance that his passion is returned, but afterwards "Love expels jealousy" (French),[2] or, at least, it ought to do so. "Love demands faith, and faith steadfastness" (Italian);[3] but too often "Love gives for guerdon jealousy and broken faith" (Italian).[4] It is an Italian woman's belief that "It is better to have a husband without love than with jealousy."[5]

No folly to being in love. — Welsh.

"To love and to be wise is impossible" (Spanish);[6] or, as an antique French proverb says, the two things have not the same abode.[7] This is the creed of those

---

[1] Qui non zelat non amat.

[2] Amour chasse jalousie.

[3] Amor vuol fede, e fede vuol fermezza.

[4] Amor dà per mercede gelosia e rotta fede.

[5] Meglio è aver il marito senza amore che con gelosia.

[6] Amar y saber, no puede ser.

[7] Aimer et savoir n'ont même manoir. [For this last word some modern collections substitute *manière*, which makes nonsense.]

who have not themselves been lovers. As Calderon
sings, in lines admirably rendered by Mr. Fitzgerald, —

> " He who far off beholds another dancing,
> Even one who dances best, and all the time
> Hears not the music that he dances to,
> Thinks him a madman, apprehending not
> The law which moves his else eccentric action ;
> So he that 's in himself insensible
> Of love's sweet influence, misjudges him
> Who moves according to love's melody ;
> And knowing not that all these sighs and tears,
> Ejaculations and impatiences,
> Are necessary changes of a measure
> Which the divine musician plays, may call
> The lover crazy, which he would not do,
> Did he within his own heart hear the tune
> Played by the great musician of the world."

They that lie down [i. e., fall sick] for love, should rise for hunger.
                                                                — *Scotch.*

The presumption being that, if they had not been too
well fed, they would not have been troubled with that
disease. " Without Ceres and Bacchus, Venus freezes "
(Latin).[1] " No love without bread and wine" (French).[2]

Old pottage is sooner heated than new made.

An old flame is sooner revived than a new one kin-
dled. "One always returns to one's first love" (French).[3]
"True love never grows hoary " (Italian).[4]

---

[1] Sine Cerere et Baccho friget Venus.
[2] Sans pain, sans vin, amour n'est rien.
[3] On revient toujours à ses premières amours.
[4] Amor vero non diventa mai canuto.

Love and light cannot be hid.

Love and a cough cannot be hid.

The French add smoke to these irrepressible things.[1]
La gale is sometimes enumerated with them; and the
Danes say, "Poverty and love are hard to hide."[2]

Love and lordship like not fellowship.

Kindness comes awill. — *Scotch.*

That is, love cannot be forced. The Germans couple
it in that respect with singing.[3] "Who would be loved
must love,"[4] say the Italians; and "Love is the very
price at which love is to be bought."[5]

Our English proverbs on love are for the most part
sarcastic or jocular, and few of them can be compared,
for grace and elevation of feeling, with those of Italy.
We have no parallels in our language for the following:
— "Love knows no measure"[6] — there are no bounds
to its trustfulness and devotion; — "Love warms more
than a thousand fires;"[7] — "He who has love in his
heart has spurs in his sides;"[8] — "Love rules without
law;"[9] — "Love rules his kingdom without a sword;"[10]

---

[1] Amour, toux, et fumée en secret ne font demeurée.

[2] Armod og Kiærlighed ere onde at dölge.

[3] Liebe und Singen lässt sich nicht zwingen.

[4] Chi vuol esser amato, convien ch'il ami.

[5] Amor è il vero prezio, per che si compra amor.

[6] Amor non conosce misura.

[7] Scalda più amore che mille fuochi.

[8] Chi ha l'amor nel petto, ha lo sprone a' franchi.

[9] Amor regge senza legge.

[10] Amor regge il suo regno senza spada.

— " Love knows not labor ; " [1] — " Love is master of all arts." [2] The French have one proverb on the sovereign might of love, [3] which they borrowed from the sublime phrase in the Song of Solomon, " Love is stronger than death ; " and another, expressed in the language of their chivalric forefathers, " Love subdues all but the ruffian's heart." [4]

Marry in haste and repent at leisure.

This proverb probably came to us from Italy ; [5] but, alas! it happens too often in all countries that " Wedlock rides in the saddle, and repentance on the croup ". (French). [6] There is a joke in the Menagiana not unlike this : — A person meeting another riding on horseback with his wife behind him, applied to him the words of Horace — " Post equitem sedet atra cura." [7] " Marriage is a desperate thing," quoth Selden. " The frogs in Æsop were extremely wise ; they had a great mind to some water, but they would not leap into the well because they could not get out again." Consider well, then, what you are about before you put yourself in a condition to hear it said, —

You have tied a knot with your tongue you cannot undo with your teeth.

Some go so far as to say that " No one marries but

---

[1] Amor non conosce travaglio.
[2] Di tutte le arti maestro è amore.
[3] Amour et mort, rien n'est plus fort.
[4] Amour soumet tout hormis cœur de félon.
[5] Chi si marita in fretta, stenta adagio.
[6] Fiançailles vont en selle, et repentailles en croupe.
[7] Black care sits behind the horseman.

repents" (French).[1] The Spaniards exclaim, in language which reminds us of the custom of Dunmow, " The bacon of paradise for the married man that has not repented !"[2]

Better wed over the mixon than over the moor.

The mixon is the heap of manure in the farmyard. The proverb means that it is better not to go far from home in search of a wife — advice as old as the Greek poet Hesiod, who has a line to this effect : " Marry, in preference to all other women, one who dwells near thee." But a more specific meaning has been assigned to the English proverb by Fuller, and after him by Ray and Disraeli. They explain it as being a maxim peculiar to Cheshire, and intended to dissuade candidates for matrimony from taking the road to London, which lies over the moorland of Staffordshire. " This local proverb," says Disraeli, " is a curious instance of provincial pride, perhaps of wisdom, to induce the gentry of that county to form intermarriages, to prolong their own ancient families and perpetuate ancient friendships between them." This is a mistake, for the proverb is not peculiar to Cheshire, or to any part of England. Scotland has it in this shape : —

Better woo o'er midden nor o'er moss.

And in Germany they give the same advice, and also assign a reason for it, saying, " Marry over the mixon,

---

[1] Nul ne se marie qui ne s'en repente.
[2] El tocino de paraíso para el casado no arrepiso.

and you will know who and what she is."[1] The same
principle is expressed in different forms in other languages, *e. g.*, "Your wife and your nag get from a neighbor" (Italian).[2] "He that goes far to marry goes to be
deceived or to deceive" (Spanish).[3] The politic Lord
Burleigh seems to have regarded this "going far to
deceive" as a very proper thing to be done for the
advancement of a man's fortune. In his "Advice to his
Son," he says, "If thy estate be good, match near home
and at leisure; if weak, far off and quickly." There is
an ugly cunning in that word *quickly*. Burleigh's advice
is quite in the spirit of the French fortune hunter's
adage, "In marriage cheat who can."[4]

He that loseth his wife and sixpence hath lost a tester.

"He that loseth his wife and a farthing hath a great
loss of his farthing" (Italian).[5] In Italy also, and in
Portugal, it is said that "Grief for a dead wife lasts to
the door;"[6] and even in Provence, the land of the
troubadours, they have a rhyme to this effect:—

"Two good days for a man in this life:
When he weds and when he buries his wife."[7]

---

[1] Heirathe über den Mist, so weisst du wer sie ist.

[2] La moglie e il ronzino piglia dal vicino.

[3] Quien lejos se va á casar, o va engañado, o va á engañar.

[4] En mariage trompe qui peut.

[5] Chi perde la moglie e un quattrino, ha gran perdita del
quattrino.

[6] Doglia di moglie morta dura fino alla porta. Dôr de mulher
morta, dura até a porta.

[7] Dous bouns jours à l'home sur terro:
Quand pren mouilho, e quand l'enterro.

Nor do the wives of Provence appear to be delighted with their conjugal lot. Having lost their youthful plumpness through the cares and toils of wedlock, they oddly declare that " If a stockfish became a widow it would fatten." ¹ A Spanish woman's opinion of matrimony is thus expressed : " ' Mother, what sort of a thing is marriage ? ' — ' Daughter, it is spinning, bearing children, and weeping.' " ²

> Better a tocher [dower] in her than wi' her. — *Scotch.*
>
> A man's best fortune or his worst is his wife.

" The day you marry you kill or cure yourself " (Spanish).³ " Use great prudence and circumspection," says Lord Burleigh to his son, " in choosing thy wife, for from thence will spring all thy future good or evil ; and it is an action of life like unto a stratagem of war, wherein a man can err but once."

> The gude or ill hap o' a gude or ill life
> Is the gude or ill choice o' a gude or ill wife. — *Scotch.*

There is a Spanish rhyme much to the same effect :

" Him that has a good wife no evil in life that may not be borne, can befall.

Him that has a bad wife no good thing in life can chance to, that good you may call." ⁴

---

1 Se uno marlusse venie veouso, serie grasso.

2 Madre, que cosa es casar ?   Ilija, hilar, parir y llorar.

3 El dia que te casas, o te matas o te sanas.

4 A quien tiene buena muger, ningun mal le puede venir, que no sea de sufrir.

A quien tiene mala muger, ningun bien le puede venir, que bien se puede decir.

Put your hand in the creel, and take out either an adder or an eel.

That's matrimony. "In buying horses and taking a wife, shut your eyes and commend yourself to God" (Italian).[1] "Marriages are not as they are made, but as they turn out" (Italian).[2]

There's but ae gude wife in the country, and ilka man thinks he's got her. — *Scotch.*

It is a pleasant delusion while it lasts, and it is not incurable. Instances of complete recovery from it are not rare.

A man may woo where he will, but must wed where he's weird. — *Scotch.*

That is, where he is fated to wed. This is exactly equivalent to the English saying, —

Marriages are made in heaven,

the meaning of which Dean Trench appears to me to mistake, when he speaks with admiration of its "religious depth and beauty." I cannot find in it a shadow of religious sentiment. It simply implies that it is not forethought, inclination, or mutual fitness that has the largest share in bringing man and wife together. More efficient than all these is the force of circumstances, or what people vaguely call chance, fate, fortune, and so forth. In the French version of the adage, "Marriages are *written* in heaven," [3] we find the special formula of

---

[1] Comprar cavalli e tor moglie, serra gli occhi e raccomandati a Dio.

[2] I matrimoni sono, non come si fanno, ma come riescono.

[3] Les mariages sont écrits dans le ciel.

Oriental fatalism; and fatalism is everywhere the popular creed respecting marriage. Hence, as Shakspeare says, —

> " The ancient saying is no heresy —
> Hanging and wiving go by destiny."

" But now consider the old proverbe to be true y saieth : that marriage is destinie." — *Hall's Chronicles.*

If marriages be made in heaven some had few friends there. — *Scotch.*

Ne'er seek a wife till ye hae a house and a fire burning. — *Scotch.*

More belongs to a bed than four bare legs.

Marriage is honorable, but housekeeping is a shrew.

Sweetheart and honey-bird keeps no house.

" Marry, marry, and what about the housekeeping?" (Portuguese).[1] " Remember," said a French lady to her son, who was about to make an imprudent match, " remember that in wedded life there is only one thing which continues every day the same, and that is the necessity of making the pot boil." " He that marries for love has good nights and bad days" (French).[2] " Before you marry have where to tarry" (Italian) ;[3] and remember that

A wee house has a wide throat.

It costs something to support a family, however small ; and " It is easier to build two hearths than always to have a fire on one" (German).[4]

---

[1] Casar, casar, e que do governo ?

[2] Qui se marie par amours, a bonnes nuits et mauvais jours.

[3] Innanzi al maritare. habbi l'habitare.

[4] Es ist leichter zwei Herde bauen, als auf einem immer Feuer haben.

'T is hard to wive and thrive both in a year.

Who weds ere he be wise shall die ere he thrive.

Happy is the wooing that is not long a-doing.

This is so far true as it discommends long engagements.

'T is time to yoke when the cart comes to the capples [i. e., horses].
— *Cheshire.*

That is, it is time to marry when the woman woos the man. This provincial word " capple " is Irish also, and is allied to, but not derived from, the Latin *caballus.* It is probably one of the few words of the ancient Celtic tongue of Britain which were adopted into the language of the Saxon conquerors.

Husbands are in heaven whose wives chide not.

Whether or not that heaven is ever found on earth is a question which each man must decide from his own experience. " He that has a wife has strife,"[1] say the French, and the Italian proverb-mongers take an unhandsome advantage of the fact that in their language the words " wife " and " woes " differ only by a letter.[2] St. Jerome declares that " Whoever is free from wrangling is a bachelor."[3]

A smoky chimney and a scolding wife are two bad companions.

The Scotch couple together " A leaky house and a scolding wife," in which they follow Solomon : " A continual dropping on a very rainy day and a contentious

---

[1] Qui femme a, noise a.

[2] Chi ha moglie, ha doglie.

[3] Qui non litigat cœlebs est.

woman are alike."[1] "It is better to dwell in a corner of the housetop than with a brawling woman in a wide house."[2]

A house wi' a reek and a wife wi' a reerd [scolding noise] will sune mak a man run to the door. — *Scotch.*

Of the continental versions of this proverb the Spanish[3] seems to me the best, and next to it the Dutch.[4]

It's a sair reek where the gude wife dings the gude man. — *Scotch.*

"A man in my country," says James Kelly, "coming out of his house with tears on his cheeks, was asked the occasion. He said 'there was a sair reek in the house :' but, upon further inquiry, it was found that his wife had beaten him." "It is a sad house where the hen crows and the cock is mute" (Spanish).[5] Though we have not this proverb in English, we have its spirit embodied in one word, HENPECKED, which is peculiar to ourselves.

The gray mare is the better horse.

The wife wears the breeches. "A hawk's marriage : the hen is the better bird" (French).[6]

Marry above your match and you get a master.

"In the rich woman's house she commands always,

---

[1] Prov. xxvii. 15.   [2] Prov. xxi. 19.

[3] Humo y gotera, y la muger parlera, echan el hombre de su casa fuera.

[4] Rook, stank, en kwaade wijven zijn die de mans uit de huizen drijven.

[5] Triste es la casa donde la gallina canta y el gallo calla.

[6] Mariage d'épervier : la femelle vaut mieux que le mâle.

and he never" (Spanish).[1]   "Who takes a wife for her dower turns his back on freedom" (French).[2]   But every married man is in this plight, for

> "He that has a wife has a master."[3]

"He that's not sensible of the truth of this proverb," says James Kelly, "may blot it out or pass it over."

> "As the good man saith, so say we :
> But as the good woman saith, so it must be."

Wedding and ill wintering tame both man and beast.

"You will marry and grow tame" (Spanish).[4]

He that marries a widow and two daughters marries three stark thieves.

He that marries a widow and two daughters has three back doors to his house.

And "The back door is the one that robs the house" (Italian).[5]

Never marry a widow unless her first husband was hanged.

Else the burden of an old Scotch song, "Ye'll never be like mine auld gudeman," will be dinned in your ears day and night.

He that marries a widow will have a dead man's head cast in his dish.

Happy is the wife who is married to a motherless son.

"Uno animo omnes socrus oderunt nurus," says

---

[1] En la casa de muger rica, ella manda siempre, y el nunca.

[2] Qui prend une femme pour sa dot a la liberté tourne le dos.

[3] In French, Qui prend femme, prend maître.

[4] Casaras y amansaras.

[5] La porta di dietro è quella che ruba la casa.

Terence; and this is the common testimony of experience in all ages and countries. "The husband's mother is the wife's devil" (German, Dutch).[1] "As long as I was a daughter-in-law I never had a good mother-in-law, and as long as I was a mother-in-law I never had a good daughter-in-law" (Spanish).[2] "The mother-in-law forgets that she was a daughter-in-law" (Spanish).[3] "She is well married who has neither mother-in-law nor sister-in-law" (Spanish).[4] Men, too, do not always regard their wives' mothers with tender affection, and some of the many bitter sayings against mothers-in-law seem to be common to both sexes. Such is this queer Ulster rhyme :

"Of all the ould women that ever I saw,
Sweet bad luck to my mother-in-law."

Also these Low German : "There is no good mother-in-law but she that wears a green gown;"[5] *i. e.*, that is covered with the turf of the churchyard; "The best mother-in-law is she on whose gown the geese feed;"[6] and this Portuguese, "If my mother-in-law dies, I will fetch somebody to flay her."[7]

---

[1] Des Mannes Mutter ist der Frau Teufel. Een mans moer is de duivel op den vloer.

[2] En quanto fue nuera, nunca tuve buena suegra, y en quanto fue suegra, nunca tuve buena nuera.

[3] No se acuerda la suegra que fue nuera.

[4] Aquella es bien casada, que no tiene suegra ni cuñada.

[5] Es ist keine gut Swigar, danne die einen grünen Rok an hat.

[6] Die beste Swigar ist die auf deren Rok die Gänse waiden.

[7] Se minha sogra more, buscare quem a estolle.

PARENTS AND CHILDREN.

Children are certain cares but uncertain comforts.

"LITTLE children and headaches — great children and heartaches" (Italian).[1] Nevertheless, "He knows not what love is that has not children" (Italian).[2]

It is a wise child that knows his own father.

Happily, as a French sage remarks, "One is always somebody's child, and that is a comfort."[3] "The child names the father; the mother knows him" (Livonian).

The mother knows best if the child be like the father.

The mither's breath is aye sweet. — *Scotch.*

This proverb, which belongs exclusively to Scotland, appears to me even more "exquisitely graceful and tender" than that German and French proverb so justly admired by Dean Trench, "Mother's truth keeps constant youth."[4] "There is no mother like the mother

---

[1] Fanciulli piccioli, dolor di testa; fanciulli grandi, dolor di cuore.

[2] Chi non ha figliuoli non sa che cosa sia amore.

[3] On est toujours le fils de quelqu'un; cela console.

[4] Muttertreu wird täglich neu. Tendresse maternelle toujours se renouvelle.

that bore us" (Spanish).[1] "The child that gets a step-mother gets a stepfather also" (Danish).[2]

> The crow thinks her own bird the fairest.

"Every mother's child is handsome" (German).[3] "No ape but swears he has the finest children" (German).[4] "If our child squints, our neighbor's child has a cast in both eyes" (Livonian).

> As the old cock crows so crows the young; *or*
> As the old cock crows the young cock learns.
>
> If the mare have a bald face the filly will have a blaze.
>
> Trot feyther, trot mither, how can foal amble? — *Scotch.*

Children generally follow the example of their parents, but imitate their faults more surely than their virtues. Thus, —

> A light-heeled mother makes a heavy-heeled daughter.

Unless the mother transfers a part of her household cares to the daughter, the latter will grow up in sloth and ignorance of good housewifery. "A tender-hearted mother rears a scabby daughter" (French, Italian).[5]

> A child may have too much of its mother's blessing.

Her foolish fondness may spoil it.

> The worst store is a maid unbestowed. — *Welsh.*

---

[1] No hay tal madre como la que pare.

[2] Det Barn der faaer Stivmoder, faaer ogsaa Stifvader.

[3] Jeder Mutter Kind ist schön.

[4] Kein Aff', er schwört, er habe die schönsten Kinder.

[5] Mère piteuse fait sa fille rogneuse. La madre pietosa fa la figliuola tignosa.

"A house full of daughters is a cellar full of sour beer" (Dutch).[1] Chaucer says, —

> "He that hath more smocks than shirts in a bucking,
> Had need be a man of good forelooking."

"Marry your son when you will, and your daughter when you can" (Spanish).[2]

> My son is my son till he's got him a wife;
> My daughter's my daughter all the days of her life.

This is a woman's calculation. She knows that a son-in-law will submit to her sway more tamely than a daughter-in-law.

Little pitchers have long ears.

"What the child hears at the fire is soon known at the minster" (French).[3]

Children and fools tell truth.

And tell it when it were better left untold. "These terrible children!" (French).[4]

Children and fools have merry lives.

They quickly forget past sorrows, and are careless of the future.

Children suck the mother when they are young, and the father when they are old.

---

[1] Een huis vol dochters is een kelder vol zuur bier.

[2] Casa el hijo quando quisieres, y la hija quando pudieres.

[3] Ce que l'enfant oit au foyer, est bientost connu jusqu'au monstier.

[4] Ces enfants terribles !

YOUTH AND AGE.

A ragged colt may make a good horse.[1]

An untoward boy may grow up into a proper man. This may be understood either in a physical or a moral sense. "There is no colt but breaks some halter" (Italian),[2] otherwise it is good for nothing (French).[3] "Youth comes back from far" (French).[4] Do not despair of it as lost, though it runs a mad gallop; something of the sort is to be expected of all but those preternaturally sedate youths who are born, as the author of "Eothen" says, with a Chifney bit in their mouths from their mother's womb.

A man at five may be a fool at fifteen.

In the days when cock-fighting was a fashionable pastime, game chickens that crowed too soon or too often were condemned to the spit as of no promise or ability. "A lad," says Archbishop Whately, "who has to a degree that excites wonder and admiration the

---

[1] Spanish : De potro sarnoso buen caballo hermoso. German : Aus klattrigen Fohlen werden die schönsten Hengste.

[2] Non c'è polledro che non rompa qualche cavezza.

[3] Rien ne vaut poulain s'il ne rompt son lien.

[4] Jeunesse revient de loin.

character and demeanor of an intelligent man of mature years, will probably be that and nothing more all his life, and will cease accordingly to be anything remarkable, because it was the precocity alone that ever made him so. It is remarked by greyhound fanciers that a well-formed, compact-shaped puppy never makes a fleet dog. They see more promise in the loose-jointed, awkward, and clumsy ones. And even so there is a kind of crudity and unsettledness in the minds of those young persons who turn out ultimately the most eminent."

Soon ripe soon rotten.

" Late fruit keeps well " (German).[1]

It is better to knit than to blossom.

Orchard trees may blossom fairly, yet bear no fruit.

It early pricks that will be a thorn.

Some indications of future character may be seen even in infancy. The child is father of the man.

Soon crooks the tree that good gambrel will be.

A gambrel (from the Italian *gamba*, a leg) is a crooked piece of wood, on which butchers hang the carcasses of beasts by the legs.

As the twig is bent the tree's inclined.

Best to bend while it is a twig.

It is not easy to straighten in the oak the crook that grew in the sapling. — *Gaelic*.

" What the colt learns in youth he continues in old

---

[1] Spät Obst liegt lange.

age" (French).[1] "What youth learns, age does not forget" (Danish).[2]

Reckless youth maks ruefu' eild. — *Scotch.*

"If youth knew! if age could!" (French).[3]

---

[1] Ce que poulain prend en jeunesse, il le continue en vieillesse.
[2] Det Ung nemmer, Gammel ei glemmer.
[3] Si jeunesse savait! si vieillesse pouvait!

NATURAL CHARACTER.

What's bred in the bone will never be out of the flesh.

WHAT is innate is not to be eradicated by force of education or self-discipline ; these may modify the outward manifestations of a man's nature, but not transmute that nature itself. What belongs to it "lasts to the grave" (Italian).[1] The ancients had several proverbs to the same purpose, such as this one, which is found in Aristophanes — "You will never make a crab walk straight forwards"— and this Latin one, which is repeated in several modern languages : "The wolf changes his coat, but not his disposition ;"[2] — he turns gray with age. The Spaniards say he "loses his teeth, but not his inclinations."[3] "What is sucked in with the mother's milk runs out in the shroud" (Spanish).[4] Horace's well-known line, —

"Naturam expellas furca tamen usque recurret" —

"Though you cast out nature with a fork, it will still return" — has very much the air of a proverb versified.

---

1 Chi l'ha per natura, fin alla fossa dura.
2 Lupus pilum mutat non mentem.
3 El lobo pierde los dientes, mas no los mientes.
4 Lo que en la leche se mama, en la mortaja se derrama.

The same thought is better expressed in a French line which has acquired proverbial currency : —

"Chassez le naturel, il revient au galop."

"Drive away nature, and back it comes at a gallop." This line is very commonly attributed to Boileau, but erroneously. The author of it is Chaulieu (?). The Orientals ascribe to Mahomet the saying, "Believe, if thou wilt, that mountains change their places, but believe not that men change their dispositions."

Cat after kind.

"What is born of a hen will scrape" (Italian).[1] "What is born of a cat will catch mice" (French, Italian).[2] This proverb is taken from the fable of a cat transformed into a woman, who scandalized her friends by jumping from her seat to catch a mouse. "A good hound hunts by kind" (French).[3] "It is kind father to him," as the Scotch say. "Good blood cannot lie" (French);[4] its generous instincts are sure to display themselves on fit occasions. On the other hand, "The son of an ass brays twice a day."[5] We need not say what people that stroke of grave humor belongs to.

Drive a cow to the ha' and she 'll run to the byre. — *Scotch.*

She will be more at home there than in the drawing-

---

[1] Chi nasce di gallina, convien che rozzuola.

[2] Chi naquit chat, court après les souris. Chi nasce di gatta sorice piglia.

[3] Bon chien chasse de race.

[4] Bon sang ne peut mentir.

[5] El hijo del asino dos veces rozna al dia.

room. " A sow prefers bran to roses " (French).[1]
" Set a frog on a golden stool, and off it hops again
into the pool " (German).[2]

There's no making a silk purse of a sow's ear;

or, " A good arrow of a pig's tail " (Spanish) ;[3] or, " A
sieve of an ass's tail " (Greek).

A carrion kite will never make a good hawk.[4]
An inch o' a nag is worth a span o' an aver. — *Scotch.*
A kindly aver will never make a good nag. — *Scotch.*

An aver is a cart horse.

One leg of a lark is worth the whole body of a kite.
A piece of a kid is worth two of a cat.
Bray a fool in a mortar, he'll be never the wiser.

" To wash an ass's head is loss of suds " (French).[5]
" The malady that is incurable is folly " (Spanish).[6]

There's no washing a blackamoor white.

" Wash a dog, comb a dog, still a dog is but a dog "
(French).[7]

A hog in armor is still but a hog.

An ape is an ape, a varlet's a varlet,
Though he be clad in silk and scarlet.

There's no getting white flour out of a coal-sack.

---

[1] Truie aime mieux bran que roses.
[2] Setz einen Frosch auf goldnen Stuhl,
    Er hupft doch wieder in den Pfuhl.
[3] De rabo de puerco nunca buen virote.
[4] On ne saurait faire d'une buse un épervier.
[5] A laver la tête d'un âne, on perd sa lessive.
[6] El mal que no se puede sañar, es locura.
[7] Lavez chien, peignez chien, toujours n'est chien que chien.

"Whatever the bee sucks turns to honey, and whatever the wasp sucks turns to venom" (Portuguese).[1]

Eagles catch no flies.

Literally translated from a Latin adage[2] much used by Queen Christina, of Sweden, who affected a superb disdain for petty details. The Romans had another proverbial expression for the same idea: "The prætor takes no heed of very small matters,"[3] for his was a superior court, and did not try cases of minor importance. Our modern lawyers have retained the classical adage, only substituting the word "law" for "prætor." They say, "De minimis non curat lex," which might, perhaps, be freely translated, "Lawyers don't stick at trifles."

---

[1] Quanto chupa a abelha, mel torna, e quanto a aranha, peçonha.

[2] Aquila non capit muscas.

[3] De minimis non curat prætor.

3

HOME.

Home is home, be it ever so homely.
Hame is a hamely word. — *Scotch.*

"HOMELY" and "hamely" are not synonymous, but
imply different ideas associated with home. The one
means plain, unadorned, fit for every-day use; the other
means familiar, pleasant, dear to the affections. "To
every bird its nest is fair" (French, Italian).[1] "East
and west, at home the best" (German).[2] "The reek of
my own house," says the Spaniard, "is better than the
fire of another's."[3] The same feeling is expressed with
less energy, but far more tenderly, in a beautiful Italian
proverb, which loses greatly by translation: "Home,
my own home, tiny though thou be, to me thou seemest
an abbey."[4] Two others in the same language are exquisitely tender: "My home, my mother's breast."[5]
How touching this simple juxtaposition of two loveliest

---

[1] A tout oiseau son nid est beau. A ogni uccello suo nido è
bello.

[2] Ost und West, daheim das Best.

[3] Mas vale humo de mi casa que fuego de la agena.

[4] Casa mia, casa mia, per piccina che tu sia, tu mi sembri una
badia.

[5] Casa mia, mamma mia.

things! Again, "Tie me hand and foot, and throw me among my own."[1]

Every cock is proud on his own dunghill.
A cock is crouse on his ain midden. — *Scotch.*

This proverb has descended to us from the Romans: it is quoted by Seneca.[2] Its medieval equivalent, *Gallus cantat in suo sterquilinio,* was probably present to the mind of the first Napoleon when, in reply to those who advised him to adopt the Gallic cock as the imperial cognizance, he said, " No, it is a bird that crows on a dunghill." The French have altered the old proverb without improving it, thus: " A dog is stout on his own dunghill."[3] The Italian is better: " Every dog is a lion at home."[4] The Portuguese give us the counterpart of this adage, saying, " The fierce ox grows tame on strange ground."[5]

An Englishman's house is his castle.

But sanitary reformers tell him truly that he has no right to shoot poisoned arrows from it at his neighbors. The French say, " The collier (or charcoal burner) is master in his own house,"[6] and refer the origin of the proverb to a hunting adventure of Francis I., which is related by Blaise de Montluc. Having outriden all his followers, the king took shelter at nightfall in the cabin

---

[1] Legami mani e piei, e gettami tra' miei.
[2] Gallus in suo sterquilinio plurimum potest.
[3] Chien sur son fumier est hardi.
[4] Ogni cane è leone a casa sua.
[5] O boi bravo na terra alheia se faz manso.
[6] Charbonnier est maître chez soi.

of a charcoal burner, whose wife he found sitting alone on the floor before the fire. She told him, when he asked for hospitality, that he must wait her husband's return, which he did, seating himself on the only chair the cabin contained. Presently the man came in, and, after a brief greeting, made the king give him up the chair, saying he was used to sit in it, and it was but right that a man should be master in his own house. Francis expressed his entire concurrence in this doctrine, and he and his host supped together very amicably on game poached from the royal forest.

" Man," said Ferdinand VII. to the Duke of Medina Celi, the premier nobleman of Spain, who was helping him on with his great coat, " man, how little you are!" "At home I am great," replied the dwarfish *grande* (grandee). "When I am in my own house I am a king " (Spanish).[1]

---

[1] Mientras en mi casa estoy, rey me soy.

PRESENCE. — ABSENCE. — SOCIAL INTERCOURSE.

Long absent, soon forgotten.
Out of sight, out of mind.

"FRIENDS living far away are no friends" (Greek). "He that is absent will not be the heir" (Latin).[1] "Absence is love's foe: far from the eyes, far from the heart" (Spanish).[2] "The dead and the absent have no friends" (Spanish).[3] "The absent are always in the wrong" (French).[4] "Absent, none without fault; present, none without excuse" (French).[5]

Against this string of proverbs, all running in one direction, we may set off the Scotch saying, —

They are aye gude that are far awa';

and this French one: "A little absence does much good."[6] Without affirming too absolutely that

---

[1] Absens hæres non erit.

[2] Ausencia enemiga de amor: quan lejos de ojo tan lejos de corazon.

[3] A muertos y a idos no hay mas amigos.

[4] Les absents ont toujours tort.

[5] Absent n'est point sans coulpe, ni présent sans excuse.

[6] Un peu d'absence fait grand bien.

Friends agree best at a distance, —

which was a proverb before Rochefoucauld wrote it down among his maxims, — we may admit that " To preserve friendship a wall must be put between " (French) ;[1] and that " A hedge between keeps friendship green " (German).[2] " Love your neighbor, but do not pull down the hedge " (German).[3] " There are certain limits of sociality, and prudent reserve and absence may find a place in the management of the tenderest relations." (*Friends in Council.*) This lesson the Spaniards embody in two proverbs, bidding you " Go to your aunt's (or your brother's) house, but not every day."[4] Friends meet with more pleasure after a short separation. " The imagination," says Montaigne, " embraces more fervently and constantly what it goes in search of than what one has at hand. Count up your daily thoughts, and you will find that you are most absent from your friend when you have him with you. His presence relaxes your attention, and gives your thoughts liberty to absent themselves at every turn and upon every occasion."

Better be unmannerly than troublesome.
I wad rather my friend should think me framet than fashious.
— *Scotch.*

That is, I would rather my friend should think me

---

[1] Pour amitié garder il faut parois entreposer.
[2] Ein Zaun dazwischen mag die Liebe erfrischen.
[3] Liebe deinen Nachbar, reiss aber den Zaun nicht ein.
[4] A casa de tu tia, mas no cada dia. A casa de tu hermano, mas no cada serano.

strange (*fremd,* German) than troublesome (*fâcheux,* French).

Too much familiarity breeds contempt.

Ower-meikle hameliness spoils gude courtesy.

Hameliness means familiarity. See "Hame is a hamely word," p. 36.

Leave welcome ahint you. — *Scotch.*

Do not outstay your welcome. "A guest and a fish stink on the third day" (Spanish).[1]

Welcome the coming, speed the parting guest.

"Aweel, kinsman," says Rob Roy to the baillie, "ye ken our fashion, — foster the guest that comes, further him that maun gang." "Let the guest go before the storm bursts" (German).[2]

If the badger leaves his hole the tod will creep into it. — *Scotch.*

"He that quits his place loses it" (French).[3] "Whoso absents himself, his share absents itself" (Arab).

---

[1] El huesped y el pece á tres dias hiede.

[2] Lass den Gast ziehen eh das Gewitter ausbricht.

[3] Qui quitte sa place la perd.

FRIENDSHIP.

He is my friend who grinds at my mill;

THAT is, who is serviceable to me, — a vile sentiment if understood too absolutely ; but the proverb is rather to be interpreted as offering a test by which genuine friendship may be distinguished from its counterfeit. " Deeds are love, and not fine speeches " (Spanish).[1] " If you love me, John, your acts will tell me so " (Spanish).[2] " In the world you have three sorts of friends," says Chamfort ; " your friends who love you, your friends who do not care about you, and your friends who hate you."

Kindness will creep where it canna gang. — *Scotch.*

It will find some way to manifest itself, in spite of all hinderances. As Burns sings, —

> " A man may hae an honest heart,
>   Though poortith hourly stare him ;
> A man may tak a neebor's part,
>   Yet no hae cash to spare him."

Friendship canna stand aye on ane side. — *Scotch.*

It demands reciprocity. " Little presents keep up

---

[1] Obras son amores, que no buenas razones.

[2] Se bien me quieres, Juan, tus obras me lo diran.

friendship" (French) ;[1] and so do mutual good offices.
Note that the French proverb speaks of *little* presents —
such things as are valued between friends, not for their
intrinsic value, but as tokens of good-will.

Before you make a friend, eat a peck of salt with him.

Take time to know him thoroughly.

Sudden friendship, sure repentance.

Never trust much to a new friend or an old enemy.

Nor even to an old friend, if you and he have once
been at enmity. "Patched-up friendship seldom becomes
whole again" (German).[2] "Broken friendship may be
soldered, but never made sound" (Spanish).[3] "A reconciled friend, a double foe" (Spanish).[4] "Beware of a
reconciled friend as of the devil" (Spanish).[5] Asmo-
deus, speaking of his quarrel with Paillardoc, says,
"They reconciled us, we embraced, and ever since we
have been mortal enemies."

Old friends and old wine are best.

"Old tunes are sweetest, and old friends are surest,"
says Claud Halcro. "Old be your fish, your oil, your
friend" (Italian).[6]

---

[1] Les petits cadeaux entretiennent l'amitié.

[2] Geflickte Freundschaft wird selten wieder ganz.

[3] Amigo quebrado soldado, mas nunca sano.

[4] Amigo reconciliado, amigo doblado.

[5] De amigo reconciliado, guarte del como del diablo. Cum
inimico nemo in gratiam tuto redit. — *Pub. Syrus.*

[6] Pesce, oglio, e amico vecchio.

One enemy is too many, and a hundred friends are too few.

Enmity is unhappily a much more active principle than friendship.

Save me from my friends!

An ejaculation often called forth by the indiscreet zeal which damages a man's cause whilst professing to serve it. The full form of the proverb — "God save me from my friends, I will save myself from my enemies " — is almost obsolete amongst us, but is found in most languages of the continent, and is applied to false friends. Bacon tells us that " Cosmos, Duke of Florence, was wont to say of perfidious friends that we read we ought to forgive our enemies ; but we do not read we ought to forgive our friends."

A full purse never lacked friends.

An empty purse does not easily find one. To say that " The best friends are in the purse " (German),[1] is, perhaps, putting the matter a little too strongly ; but, at all events, " Let us have florins, and we shall find cousins " (Italian).[2] " The rich man does not know who is his friend."[3] This Gascon proverb may be taken in a double sense : the rich man's friends are more than he can number; he cannot be sure of the sincerity of any of them. " He who is everybody's friend is either very poor or very rich " (Spanish).[4] " Now that I have a ewe and

---

1 Die beste Freunde stecken im Beutel.
2 Abbiamo pur fiorini, che trovaremo cugini.
3 Riché homé non sap qui ly es amyg.
4 Quien te todos es amigo, ó es muy pobre, ó es muy rico.

a lamb everybody says to me, 'Good day, Peter'"
(Spanish).[1] Everybody looks kindly on the thriving man.

A friend in need is a friend indeed.

But, as such friends are rare, the Scotch proverb
counsels not amiss, —

Try your friend afore ye need him.

On the other hand, "He that would have many
friends should try few of them" (Italian).[2] "Let him
that is wretched and beggared try everybody, and then
his friend" (Italian).[3]

A friend is never known till one have need.

"A friend cannot be known in prosperity, and an
enemy cannot be hidden in adversity" (Ecclesiasticus).
"A sure friend is known in a doubtful case" (Ennius).[4]

When good cheer is lacking, friends will be packing.

"The bread eaten, the company departed" (Spanish).[5]
"While the pot boils, friendship blooms" (German).[6]

"In time of prosperity friends will be plenty ;
In time of adversity not one in twenty."

No longer foster, no longer friend.
Help yourself, and your friends will like you.

"Give out that you have many friends, and believe

---

[1] Ahora que tengo oveja y borrego, todos me dicen : En hora
buena estais, Pedro.

[2] Chi vuol aver amici assai, ne provi pochi.

[3] Chi è misero e senza denari, provi tutti, e poi l'amico.

[4] Amicus certus in re incerta cernitur.

[5] El pan comido, la compañia deshecha.

[6] Siedet der Topf, so blühet die Freundschaft.

that you have few" (French).[1] By that means you will
not expose yourself to be bitterly disappointed, and you
will secure the favors which the world is ready to bestow
on those who seem to have least need of them.

> A friend at court is better than a penny in the purse.
> Kissing goes by favor.

Every one makes it his business to "Take care of
Dowb." "They are rich," therefore, "who have friends"
(Portuguese, Latin).[2] "It is better to have friends on
the market than money in one's coffer" (Spanish).[3]
Every one dances as he has friends in the ball-room"
(Portuguese).[4] "There's no living without friends"
(Portuguese).[5]

---

[1] Il faut se dire beaucoup d'amis, et s'en croire peu.
[2] Aquellos saō ricos que tem amigos. Ubi amici, ibi opes.
[3] Mas valen amigos en la plaça que dineros en el arca.
[4] Cada hum dança como tem os amigos na sala.
[5] Naō se pode viver sem amigos.

CO-OPERATION.—RECIPROCITY.— SUBORDINATION.

One beats the bush and another catches the birds.

Sic vos non vobis. The proverb is derived from an old way of fowling by torchlight in the winter nights. A man walks along a lane, carrying a bush smeared with birdlime and a lighted torch. He is preceded by another, who beats the hedges on both sides and starts the birds, which, flying towards the light, are caught by the limed twigs. An imprudent use of this proverb by the Duke of Bedford, regent of France during the minority of our Henry VI., has given it historical celebrity. When the English were besieging Orleans, the Duke of Burgundy, their ally, intimated his desire that the town, when taken, should be given over to him. The regent replied, " Shall I beat the bush and another take the bird ? No such thing." These words so offended the duke that he deserted the English at a time when they had the greatest need of his help to resist the efforts of Charles VII.

Here the proverb was used to imply an unfair division of spoil, or what was called, in the duchy of Bretragne, " A Montgomery distribution — all on one side, and

nothing on the other."[1] (The powerful family of Montgomery were in the habit of taking the lion's share).
It may also be applied to the manner in which confed-
erates play into each other's hands. "The dog that
starts the hare is as good as the one that catches it"
(German).[2]

The receiver is as bad as the thief.

"He sins as much who holds the sack as he who puts
into it" (French).[3] "He who holds the ladder is as bad
as the burglar" (German).[4]

Lie for him and he'll swear for you.
Speir at Jock Thief if I be a leal man. — Scotch.

"Ask my comrade, who is as great a liar as myself"
(French).[5]

The lion had need of the mouse.

The grateful mouse in the fable rescued her bene-
factor from the toils by gnawing the cords. "Soon or
late the strong needs the help of the weak" (French).[6]
"Every ten years one man has need of another"
(Italian).[7]

---

[1] Partage de Montgomery — tout d'un coté, rien de l'autre ;
like "Irish reciprocity, all on one side."

[2] Der Hund, der den Hasen ausspürt, ist so gut wie der ihn
fängt.

[3] Autant pèche celui qui tient le sac que celui qui met dedans.

[4] Wer die Leiter hält, ist so schuldig wie der Dieb.

[5] Demandez-le à mon compagnon, qui est aussi menteur que
moi.

[6] Ou tôt ou tard, ou près ou loin,
    Le fort du faible a besoin.

[7] Ogni dieci anni un uomo ha bisogno dell' altro.

Two to one are odds at football.

"Not Hercules himself could resist such odds" (Latin).[1] "Three helping each other are as good as six" (Spanish).[2] "Three brothers, three castles" (Italian).[3] "Three, if they unite against a town, will ruin it" (Arab).

When two ride the same horse one must ride behind.

And, furthermore, he must be content to journey as the foremost man pleases. "He who rides behind does not saddle when he will" (Spanish).[4] The question of precedence is settled in this case by another English proverb:

He that hires the horse must ride before.

The man who hires or owns the horse is Capital, and Labor must ride behind him. In other cases the question will often have to be decided by force.

You stout and I stout, who shall carry the dirt out?

"You a lady, I a lady, who is to drive out the sow?" (Gallegan).[5]

Tarry breeks pays no fraught. — *Scotch.*

Pipers don't pay fiddlers.

"One barber shaves another" (French).[6] "One

---

[1] Ne Hercules contra duos.

[2] Ayudándose tres, para peso de seis.

[3] Tre fratelli, tre castelli.

[4] Quien tras otro cabalga, no ensella quando quiere.

[5] Vos dona, yo dona, quen botará a porca foro ?

[6] Un barbier rase l'autre.

hand washes the other " (Greek).[1] " One ass scratches another " (Latin).[2]

> Ka me, ka thee. — *Scotch.*
> Turn about is fair play.
> Giff-gaff is good fellowship.
> Like master like man.

" The beadle of the parish is always of the opinion of his reverence the vicar " (French).[3]

---

[1] Χειρ χειρα νιπτει.

[2] Asinus asinum fricat.

[3] Le bedeau de la paroisse est toujours de l'avis de monsieur le curé.

LUCK. — FORTUNE. — MISFORTUNE.

Luck is all.

A DESPERATE doctrine, based on that one-sided view of human affairs which is expressed in Byron's parody of a famous passage in Addison's *Cato:*

> " 'T is not in mortals to command success ;
> But do you more, Sempronius, — *don't* deserve it ;
> And, take my word, you 'll have no jot the less."

"The worst pig gets the best acorn" (Spanish).[1] "A good bone never falls to a good dog" (French) ;[2] and "The horses eat oats that don't earn them" (German).[3] But this last proverb has also another application. "Other rules may vary," says Sydney Smith, "but this is the only one you will find without exception, — that in this world the salary or reward is always in the inverse ratio of the duties performed."

The more rogue the more luck.
The devil's children have the devil's luck.

But their prosperity is false and fleeting. "The devil's meal runs half to bran" (French).[4]

---

[1] Al mas ruin puerco la mejor bellota.
[2] A un bon chien n'échet jamais un bon os.
[3] Die Rosse fressen den Haber die ihn nicht verdienen.
[4] La farine du diable s'en va moitié en son.

God sends fools fortune.

It is to this version of the Latin adage, *Fortuna favet fatuis* ("Fortune favors fools"), that *Touchstone* alludes in his reply to *Jacques:*

> " 'No sir,' quoth he;
> 'Call me not fool till Heaven hath sent me fortune.' "

The Spaniards express this popular belief by a striking figure: "The mother of God appears to fools."[1] The Germans say, "Fortune and women are fond of fools ;"[2] and the converse of this holds good likewise, since "Fortune makes a fool of him whom she too much favors" (Latin) ;[3] and so do women sometimes. When we consider how much what is called success in life depends on getting into one of "the main grooves of human affairs," we can account for the common remark that blockheads thrive better in the world than clever people, and that "Jack gets on by his stupidity" (German).[4] "It is all the difference of going by railway and walking over a ploughed field, whether you adopt common courses or set up one for yourself," — which is most likely to be done by people of superior abilities. "You will see . . . . . most inferior persons highly placed in the army, in the church, in office, at the bar. They have somehow got upon the line, and have moved on well, with very little original motive powers of their own. Do not let this make you talk as if merit were

---

[1] A los bobos se les aparece la madre de Dios.
[2] Glück und Weiber haben die Narren lieb.
[3] Fortuna nimium quem favet stultum facit.
[4] Hans kommt durch seine Dummheit fort.

utterly neglected in these or other professions, only
that getting well into the groove will frequently do instead of any great excellence."[1] With this explanation
we are prepared to admit that there is some reason in
the Spanish adage, " God send you luck, my son, and
little wit will serve your turn."[2]

> It is better to be lucky than wise.
> It is better to be born lucky than rich.
> Hap and ha'penny is warld's gear eneuch. — *Scotch.*

" The lucky man's bitch litters pigs " (Spanish).[3]

> Happy go lucky.
> The happy [lucky] man canna be harried. — *Scotch.*

The lucky man cannot be ruined. Seeming disasters
will often prove to be signal strokes of good fortune for
him. Such a man will have cause to say, " The ox
that tossed me threw me upon a good place"(Spanish).[4]

> He is like a cat, he always falls on his feet.
> Cast ye owre the house riggen, and ye'll fa' on your feet. — *Scotch.*
> Give a man luck, and throw him into the sea.

" Pitch him into the Nile," say the Arabs, "and he
will come up with a fish in his mouth;" and the Germans, "If he threw up a penny on the roof, down
would come a dollar to him."[5]

> What is worse than ill luck?

---

1 " Companions of my Solitude."
2 Ventura te dé Dios, hijo, que poco saber te basta.
3 A quien Dios quiere bien, la perra le pare lechones.
4 El buey que me acornó, en buen lugar me echo
5 Würf er einen Groschen aufs Dach, fiel ihm ein Thaler herunter.

An unhappy man's cart is eith to tumble. — *Scotch.*

That is, easily upset. It happens always to some people, as Coleridge said of himself, to have their bread
and butter fall on the˙buttered side. An Irishman of
this ill-starred class is commonly supposed to have been
the author of the saying,

**He that is born under a threepenny planet will never be worth a
groat.**

**If my father had made me a hatter men would have been born
without heads.**

But the thought is not original in our language: an
unlucky Arab had long ago declared, "If I were to
trade in winding-sheets no one would die." A man of
this stamp "Falls on his back and breaks his nose"
(French).[1] The Basques say of him, "Maggots breed
in his salt-box;" the Provençals, "He would sink a
ship freighted with crucifixes;" the Italians, "He
would break his neck upon a straw."[2]

Misfortunes seldom come single.

Misfortunes come by forties. — *Welsh.*

Ill comes upon waur's back. — *Scotch.*

"Fortune is not content with crossing any man once,"
says Publius Syrus.[3] "After losing, one loses roundly,"
say the French.[4] The Spaniards have three remarkable
proverbs to express the same conviction: "Whither
goest thou, Misfortune? To where there is more."[5]

---

[1] Il tombe sur le dos, et se casse le nez.

[2] Si romperebbe il collo in un filo di paglia

[3] Fortuna obesse nulli contenta est semel.

[4] Après perdre, perd-on bien.

[5] Adonde vas, mal? Adonde mas hay.

"Whither goest thou, Sorrow? Whither I am wont."[1]
"Welcome, Misfortune, if thou comest alone."[2] The
Italian equivalents are numerous: *e. g.*, "One ill calls
another."[3] "One misfortune is the eve of another."[4]
"A misfortune and a friar are seldom alone."[5]

It can't rain but it pours.

Good fortune, as well as bad, is said to come in floods.
"If the wind blows it enters at every crevice" (Arab).

It is an ill wind that blows nobody good.

There is a local version of this proverb:

It is an ill wind that blows no good to Cornwall.

On the rock-bound coasts of that shire almost any wind
brought gain to the wreckers. We have seen it somewhere alleged that the general proverb grew out of the
local one; but this is certainly not the fact, for the
former exists in other languages. Its Italian equivalent[6]
agrees closely with it in form as well as in spirit. The
French say, "Misfortune is good for something;[7]" the
Spaniards, "There is no ill but comes for good:"[8] and
"I broke my leg, perhaps for my good."[9]

Our worst misfortunes are those that never befall us.

---

1 Ado vas, duelo? Ado suelo.
2 Bien vengas, mal, si vienes solo.
3 Un mal chiama l'otro.
4 Un mal è la vigilia dell' altro.
5 Un male e un frate di rado soli.
6 Cattivo è quel vento che a nessuno è prospero.
7 A quelque chose malheur est bon.
8 No hay mal que por bien no venga.
9 Quebreme el pie, quiza por bien.

"Never give way to melancholy: nothing encroaches
more. I fight vigorously. One great remedy is to take
short views of life. Are you happy now? Are you
likely to remain so till this evening? or next week? or
next month? or next year? Then why destroy present happiness by a distant misery which may never
come at all, or you may never live to see? For every
substantial grief has twenty shadows, and most of them
shadows of your own making." — *Sydney Smith.*

> Ye're fleyed [frightened] o' the day ye ne'er saw. — *Scotch.*
> You cry out before you are hurt.
> Never yowl till you're hit. — *Ulster.*
> Let your trouble tarry till its own day comes.
> Sufficient for the day is the evil thereof.

In French, "À chaque jour suffit sa peine," words
which were frequently in Napoleon's mouth at St.
Helena. An eastern proverb says, "He is miserable
once who feels it, but twice who fears it before it comes."

> When bale is highest, boot is nighest.

"Bale" is obsolete as a substantive, but retains a
place in current English as the root of the adjective
"baleful." The proverb means that

> When the night's darkest the day's nearest.
> The darkest hour is that before dawn.
> When things come to the worst they'll mend.

They must change, for that is the law of nature, and
any change in them must be for the better. Thus,
"By dint of going wrong all will come right" (French).[1]

---

[1] À force de mal aller tout ira bien.

"Ill is the eve of well" (Italian) ;[1] and "It is at the narrowest part of the defile that the valley begins to open" (Persian). " When the tale of bricks is doubled Moses comes" (Hebrew).

He that's down, down with him.

Such is the way of the world — " the oppressed oppressing." " Him that falls all the world run over" (German).[2] " He that has ill luck gets ill usage" (Old French).[3] "All bite the bitten dog" (Portuguese).[4] " When a dog is drowning everybody brings him drink" (French).[5]

Knock a man down, and kick him for falling.

A sort of treatment like what they call in France "The custom of Lorris : the beaten pay the fine."[6] It was enacted by the charter of Lorris in the Orléanais, conferred by Philip the Fair, that any man claiming to have money due to him from another, but unable to produce proof of the debt, might challenge the alleged debtor to a judicial combat with fists. The beaten combatant had judgment given against him, which always included a fine to the lord of the manor.

The puir man is aye put to the warst. — *Scotch.*

" The ill-clad to windward" (French).[7]

---

1 Il male è la vigilia del bene.
2 Wer da fallt, über ihm laufen alle Welt.
3 A qui il meschet, on lui meffaict.
4 Ao caō mordido, todos o mordem.
5 Quand le chien se noye, toute le monde lui porte à boire.
6 Coutume de Lorris ; les battus payent l'amende.
7 Les mal vêtus devers le vent.

The weakest goes to the wall,

which is the worst place in a crowd and a crush. Also,

Where the dyke is lowest men go over.

" Where the dam is lowest the water first runs over "
(Dutch).[1] People overrun and oppress those who are
least able to resist.

When the tree falls every man goes with his hatchet.

" When the tree is down everybody gathers wood "
(Latin).[2] " If my beard is burnt, others try to light
their pipes at it " (Turkish).

Where the carcass is, the eagles will be gathered together.

" ' We are, then, irremediably ruined, Mr. Oldbuck ? '
(The speaker is Miss Wardour, in the ' Antiquary.')

" ' Irremediably ? I hope not; but the instant demand
is very large, and others will doubtless pour in.'

" ' Ay, never doubt that, Monkbarns,' said Sir Arthur ;
' where the slaughter is, the eagles will be gathered
together. I am like a sheep which I have seen fall
down a precipice, or drop down from sickness : if you
had not seen a single raven or hooded crow for a fort-
night before, he will not be on the heather ten minutes
before half a dozen will be pecking out his eyes (and he
drew his hand over his own), and tearing out his heart-
strings before the poor devil has time to die.' "

Put your finger in the fire and say it was your fortune. — *Scotch.*

Blame yourself only for the consequences of your

---

[1] Waar de dam het laagst is, loopt het water het eerst over.
[2] Arbore dejectâ quivis colligit ligna.

own folly. Edgar, in *Lear*, says, " This is the excellent foppery of the world ! That when we are sick in fortune we make guilty of our disasters, the sun, the moon, and the stars ; as if we were villains on necessity ; fools by heavenly compulsion ; knaves, thieves, and treachers by spherical predominance ; drunkards, liars, and adulterers by a forced obedience of planetary influence ; and all that we are evil in by a divine thrusting on : an admirable evasion ! "

FORETHOUGHT.— CARE.— CAUTION.

Look before you leap.
Don't buy a pig in a poke.

A POKE is a pouch or bag. The word, which is still current in the northern counties of England, corresponds to the French *poche*, as "pocket" does to the diminutive, *pochette*. *Bouge* and *bougette* are other forms of the same word ; and from these we get "budget," which, curiously enough, has gone back from us to its original owners with a newly-acquired meaning ; for the French Minister of Finance presents his annual Budget like our own Chancellor of the Exchequer. The French say, *Acheter chat en poche:* "To buy a cat in a poke," or game bag ; and the meaning of that proverb is explained by this other one, "To buy a cat for a hare."[1] So also the Dutch,[2] the Italian,[3] etc. The pig of the English proverb is chosen for the sake of the alliteration at some sacrifice of sense.

No safe wading in unknown waters.

Therefore, "Swim on, and trust them not" (French).[4]

---

[1] Acheter le chat pour le lièvre.
[2] Een kat in een zak koopen.
[3] Non comprar gatta in sacco.
[4] Nage toujours, er ne t'y fie pas.

"Who sees not the bottom, let him not pass the water" (Italian).[1]

> Beware of had I wist.
> "Had I wist," quoth the fool.

"It is the part of a fool to say, 'I should not have thought it'" (Latin).[2]

> Stretch your arm no farther than your sleeve will reach.
> Never put out your arm further than you can easily draw it back again.

Cautious Nicol Jarvie attributes to neglect of this rule the commercial difficulties of his correspondent, Mr. Osbaldistone, "a gude honest gentleman; but I aye said he was ane of them wad make a spune or spoil a horn." Perhaps it is to ridicule the folly of attempting things beyond the reach of our powers that the Germans tell us, "Asses sing badly because they pitch their voices too high."[3]

> Measure twice, cut but once.

An irrevocable act should be well considered beforehand. Dean Trench quotes this as a Russian proverb, but it is to be found in James Kelly's Scottish collection, and is common to many European languages.

> Second thoughts are best.

Therefore it is well to "take counsel of one's pillow." "The morning is wiser than the evening" (Russian), sometimes because — in Russia especially — the evening

---

[1] Chi non vede il fondo, non passa l'acqua.
[2] Stulti est dicere non putârim.
[3] Esel singen schlecht, weil sie zu hoch anstimmen.

is drunk and the morning is sober, but generally because
the night affords time for reflection. " The night brings
counsel" (French, Latin, German).[1] "Night is the
mother of thoughts" (Italian).[2] "Sleep upon it, and
you will take counsel" (Spanish).[3]

> Raise nae mair deils than ye can lay.— *Scotch.*
>
> Do not rip up old sores.

"Nor stir up an evil that has been fairly buried"
(Latin).[4]

> Don't wake a sleeping dog.

" When misfortune sleeps let no one wake her"
(Spanish).[5]

> To lock the stable door when the steed is stolen.

" The wise Italians," says Poor Richard [Benjamin
Franklin], "make this proverbial remark on our nation:
'The English feel, but they do not see;' that is, they
are sensible of inconveniences when they are present,
but do not take sufficient care to prevent them; their
natural courage makes them too little apprehensive of
danger, so that they are often surprised by it unpro-
vided with the proper means of security. When it is
too late they are sensible of their imprudence. After
great fires they provide buckets and engines; after a

---

[1] La nuit porte conseil.   In nocte consilium.   Guter Rath
kommt über Nacht.

[2] La notte è la madre di piensieri.

[3] Dormireis sobre ello, y tomareis acuerdo.

[4] Malum bene conditum ne moveris.

[5] Quando la mala ventura se duerme, nadie la despierte.

pestilence they think of keeping clean their streets and common sewers; and when a town has been sacked by their enemies they provide for its defence," etc. Other nations have their share of this after-wisdom, as their proverbs testify: e. g., "To cover the well when the child is drowned" (German).[1] "To stop the hole when the mischief is done" (Spanish).[2] "When the head is broken the helmet is put on" (Italian).[3] The Chinese give this good advice: "Dig a well before you are thirsty." Be prepared for contingencies.

Be bail and pay for it.
Afttimes the cautioner pays the debt. — *Scotch.*

"He that becomes responsible pays" (French).[4] "Whoso would know what he is worth let him never be a surety" (Italian).[5]

In trust is treason.

"In this world," said Lord Halifax, "men must be saved by their want of faith." "He will never prosper who readily believes" (Latin).[6] "Trust was a good man; Trust not was a better" (Italian).[7]

He should hae a lang-shafted spune that sups kail wi' the deil.
— *Scotch.*
A fidging [skittish] mare should be weel girthed. — *Scottish.*

---

[1] Den Brunnen decken so das Kind ertrunken ist.
[2] Recebido ya el daño, atapar el horado.
[3] Rotta la testa, se mette la celata.
[4] Qui répond, paye.
[5] Qui vuol saper quel che il suo sia, non faccia mai malleveria.
[6] Nequaquam recte faciet qui cito credit.
[7] Fidati era un buon uomo. Nontifidare era meglio.

A cunning, tricky fellow should be dealt with very cautiously. "A thief does not always thieve, but be always on your guard against him " (Russian).

Fast bind, fast find.

Shylock adds, "A proverb never stale to thrifty mind." "Who ties well, unties well" (Spanish).[1] "Better is a turn of the key than a friar's conscience " (Spanish).[2]

Grin when ye bind, and laugh when ye loose. — *Scotch.*

Tie the knot tightly, grin with the effort of pulling, and when you come to untie it you will smile with satisfaction, finding it has kept all safe.

Quoth the young cock, "I 'll neither meddle nor make."

He had seen the old cock's neck wrung for taking part with his master, and the hen's for taking part with his dame.

---

[1] Quien bien ata, bien desata.
[2] Mas val vuelta de clave que conciencia de frate.

PATIENCE.—FORTITUDE.—PER-SEVERANCE.

Patience and posset drink cure all maladies.
Patience is a plaster for all sores.

WE trace this proverb in an exquisite passage from "honest old Decker," as Hazlitt fondly calls him.

"*Duke.* What comfort do you find in being so calm?
Candido. That which green wounds receive from sovereign balm.
Patience, my lord! why, 't is the soul of peace;
Of all the virtues 't is nearest kin to heaven:
It makes men look gods. The best of men
That e'er wore earth about him was a sufferer,
A soft, meek, patient, humble, tranquil spirit,—
The first true gentleman that ever breathed.
The stock of patience, then, cannot be poor;
All it desires it has: what award more?
It is the greatest enemy to strife
That can be, for it doth embrace all wrongs,
And so chains up lawyers' and women's tongues.
'T is the perpetual prisoner's liberty,—
His walks and orchards; 't is the bondslave's freedom,
And makes him seem proud of his iron chain,
As though he wore it more for state than pain;
It is the beggar's music, and thus sings—
Although their bodies beg, their souls are kings.

O my dread liege! it is the sap of bliss
Bears us aloft, makes men and angels kiss;
And last of all, to end a household strife,
It is the honey 'gainst a waspish wife."

"Patience, time, and money overcome everything"
(Italian).[1] "He who does not tire, tires adversity"
(French).[2] "A stout heart breaks ill luck" (Spanish).[3]
"The remedy for hard times is to have patience"
(Arab).

Blaw the wind ne'er sae fast, it will lown at the last. — *Scotch.*
After a storm comes a calm.

"After rain comes fine weather" (French).[4]

The longest day will have an end.
Time and the hour run through the longest day.
Be the day ne'er so long, at last comes even-song.[5]

"The day will be long, but there will be an end to
it,"[6] said Damiens of that dreadful day which was to
witness his death by tortures, which are the eternal
disgrace of the French monarchy.

When one door shuts another opens.

When baffled in one direction a man of energy will
not despair, but will find another way to his object.

---

1 Pazienza, tempo e denari vincono ogni cosa.
2 Qui ne se lasse pas lasse l'adversitié.
3 Buen corazon quebranta mala ventura.
4 Après la pluie vient le beau temps.
5 Il n'est si long jour qui ne vienne à vêpres. Non vien di che
non venga sera.
6 La journée sera longue, mais elle finira.

There is more than one yew bow in Chester.

A' the keys of the country hang na in ae belt. — *Scotch.*

" There are hills beyond Pentland, and streams beyond Forth ;
If there 's lairds in the lowlands, there 's chiefs in the north ;
There are wild duinewassels three thousand times three,
Will cry hoich for the bonnet of Bonny Dundee ! "

It is a sore battle from which none escape.

One may suffer a great loss, and yet not be totally
ruined.   •

There 's as good fish in the sea as ever was caught.

A consolatory reflection for those who have missed a
good haul. The question is, will they have industry
and skill to do better another time? " If I have lost
the rings, here are the fingers still," is a stout-hearted
saying of the Italians and Spaniards.[1]

He that weel bides weel betides. — *Scotch.*

He that waits patiently comes off well at last, for
" All comes right for him who can wait " (French).[2]
" Sit down and dangle your legs, and you will see your
revenge " (Italian) ;[3] that is, time will bring you rep-
aration and satisfaction. " The world is his who has
patience " (Italian).[4] " The world belongs to the phleg-
matic " (Italian).[5] " Have patience, Cossack ; thou
wilt come to be hetman " (Russian).

---

[1] Se ben ho perso l'anello, ho pur anche le dite. Si se perdie-
ron los anillos, aqui quedaron los dedillos.

[2] Tout vient à point à qui sait attendre.

[3] Siedi e sgambetta, vedrai la tua vendetta.

[4] Il mondo è di chi ha pazienza.

[5] Il mondo è dei flemmatici.

Set a stout heart to a stae brae [a steep hillside]. — *Scotch.*
Set hard heart against hard hap.

Go about a difficult business resolutely; confront adversity with fortitude.

"Tu ne cede malis, sed contra audentior ito.
Quam tua te fortuna sinit."

That you may not be easily discouraged, the French remind you that "One may go far after he is tired."[1]

He that tholes [endures] overcomes. — *Scotch.*
The toughest skin holds longest out. — *Cumberland.*

"He conquers who sticks in his saddle" (Italian).[2] "Hard pounding, gentlemen," said Wellington at Waterloo; "but we will see who will pound the longest." "Perseverance kills the game" (Spanish).[3]

Constant dropping wears the stone.[4]
A mouse in time may bite in two a cable.

"With time and straw meddlers ripen" (French).[5] "With time a mulberry leaf becomes satin" (Chinese).

A rolling stone gathers no moss.

This is an exact rendering of an ancient Greek adage, which is repeated with little variation in most modern languages. The Italians say, "A tree often transplanted is never loaded with fruit."[6]

---

1 On va loin après qu'on est las.
2 Vince chi riman in sella.
3 Porfia mata la caza.
4 Gutta cavat lapidem non vi sed sæpe cadendo.
5 Avec du temps et de la paille les nèfles mûrissent.
6 Albero spesso traspiantato mai di frutti è caricato.

A man may bear till his back breaks.
All lay load on the willing horse.

Patience may be abused. "Through much enduring come things that cannot be endured" (Latin).[1] "Make thyself a sheep, and the wolf is ready" (Russian). "Make yourself an ass, and you'll have every man's sack on your back" (German).[2] "If you let them lay the calf on your back it will not be long before they clap on the cow" (Italian).[3] "Who lets one sit on his shoulders shall presently have him sit on his head" (German).[4] "The horse that pulls at the collar is always getting the whip" (French).[5]

Daub yourself with honey, and you'll be covered with flies.

"The gentle ewe is sucked by every lamb" (Italian).[6]

---

[1] Patiendo multa veniunt quæ neques pati. — *Publius Syrus.*

[2] Wer sich zum Esel macht, dem will jeder seinen Sack auflegen.

[3] Se ti lasci metter in spalla il vitello, quindi a poco ti metteran la vacca.

[4] Wer sich auf der Achsel sitzen lässt, dem sitzt man nachher auf dem Kopf.

[5] On touche toujours sur le cheval qui tire.

[6] Pecora mansueta d'ogni agnello è tettata.

INDUSTRY AND IDLENESS.

No pains, no gains.
No sweat, no sweet.
No mill, no meal.

FROM the Latin, "Qui vitat molam, vitat farinam."
"To stop the hand is the way to stop the mouth"
(Chinese).

He that wad eat the kernel maun crack the nut. — *Scotch.*
He that gapes till he be fed will gape till he be dead.
Naethin is got without pains but dirt and lang nails. — *Scotch.*

"Good luck enters by dint of cuffs" (Spanish).[1]
Success in life is only to be won by hard striving.

"The nimble runner courses Fortune down,
And then he banquets, for she feeds the brave."

An idle brain's the deil's smiddy. — *Scotch.*
An idle brain's the devil's workshop.

"By doing nothing we learn to do mischief" (Latin).[2]
"He that labors is tempted by one devil, he that is idle
by a thousand" (Italian).[3]

---

[1] A puñadas entran las buenas hadas.
[2] Nihil agendo male agere discimus.
[3] Chi fatica è tentato da un demonio, chi sta in ozio da mille.

Idle dogs worry sheep.
Sloth is the key of poverty.
Lazy folks take the most pains.

" The dog in the kennel barks at his fleas; the dog that hunts does not feel them " (Chinese).

Who so busy as he that has nothing to do?

The Italians compare such a one to a pig's tail, that is going all day, and by night has done nothing.

Seldom lies the deil dead by the dyke side. — *Scotch.*

You are not to expect that difficulties and dangers will vanish without any effort of your own.

THRIFT.

Cut your coat according to your cloth.

Let your expenditure be proportioned to your means. "Let every one stretch his leg according to his coverlet" (Spanish).[1] "According to the arm be the blood-letting" (French).[2] "Meditating upon general improvement, I often think a great deal about the climate in these parts of the world; and I see that, without much husbandry of our means and resources, it is difficult for us to be anything but low barbarians. The difficulty of living at all in a cold, damp, destructive climate is great. Socrates went about with very scanty clothing, and men praise his wisdom in caring so little for the goods of this life. He ate sparingly, and of mean food. That is not the way, I suspect, that we can make a philosopher here. There are people who would deride me for saying this, and would contend that it gives too much weight to worldly things. But I suspect they are misled by notions borrowed from eastern climates. Here we must make prudence one of the substantial virtues." — (*Companions of my Solitude*.)

---

[1] Cada uno estiende la pierna como tiene la cubierta.

[2] Selon le bras la saignée.

A good bargain is a pickpurse.

Buy what you have no need of, and ere long you will sell your necessaries. "At a good bargain bethink you" (Italian).[1] "What is not needed is dear at a farthing" (Latin).[2] This very sensible proverb was bequeathed to us by the elder Cato; and a wiser man than Cato — Sydney Smith — has said, " If you want to make much of a small income, always ask yourself these two questions: first, do I really want it? secondly, can I do without it? These two questions, answered honestly, will double your fortune."

Silks and satins, scarlet and velvets, put out the kitchen fire.
Fools make feasts, and wise men eat them.

One of the neatest repartees ever made was that which Shaftesbury administered at the feast at which he entertained the Duke of York (James II.). He overheard Lauderdale whispering the duke, " Fools make feasts, and wise men eat them." Ere the sound of the last word had died away, Shaftesbury, responding both to the words and the sense, said, "Witty men make jests, and fools repeat them." "A fat kitchen has poverty for a neighbor" (Italian).[3] "A fat kitchen, a lean will" (German).[4]

Waste not, want not.
Wilful waste makes woeful want.
A small leak will sink a great ship.

---

[1] A buona derrata pensavi su.
[2] Quod non opus est, asse carum est.
[3] A grassa cucina povertà è vicina.
[4] Fette Küche, magere Erbschaft.

Take care of the pence, and the pounds will take care of themselves.

A fool and his money are soon parted.

He that gets his gear before his wit will be short while master of it.
— *Scotch.*

Gear is easier gained than guided.

A fool may make money, but it needs a wise man to spend it.

"Men," says Fielding (and he was an example of the truth he asserted), "do not become rich by what they get, but by what they keep." "Saving is the first gain" (Italian).[1] "Better is rule than rent" (French).[2]

A penny saved is a penny got.

The best is cheapest.

"One cannot have a good pennyworth of bad ware" (French).[3] "Much worth never cost little" (Spanish).[4] "Cheap bargains are dear" (Spanish).[5]

Miser's money goes twice to market.
Keep a thing seven years and you'll find a use for it.
Store is no sore.[6]

"He that buys by the pennyworth keeps his own house and another man's" (Italian).[7] Partly for this reason it is that

A poor man's shilling is but a penny.

---

[1] Lo sparagno è lo primo guadagno.

[2] Mieux vaut règle que rente.

[3] On n'a jamais bon marché de mauvaise marchandise.

[4] Nunca mucho costó poco.

[5] Lo barato es caro.

[6] Abondance de bien ne nuit pas.

[7] Chi vive a minuto fa le spese a' suoi e agli altri.

A toom [empty] pantry makes a thriftless gudewife. — *Scotch.*

Bare walls make giddy housewives.[1]

All is not gain that is put into the purse.

What the goodwife spares the cat eats.

There was a wife that kept her supper for her breakfast, an' she was dead or day. — *Scotch.*

---

[1] Vuides chambres font folles dames.

MODERATION. — EXCESS.

Enough is enough of bread and cheese.
Enough is as good as a feast.

"A bird can roost on but one branch; a mouse can drink no more than its fill from a river" (Chinese). "He is rich enough who does not want" (Italian).[1] But the difficulty. is to determine to a nicety the point at which there is neither want nor surplus. Practically there is no such point, however it may exist in theory; for,

There's never enough where nought is left.
Of enough men leave.

Where all is eaten up it is pretty certain that the commons were but short. "There is not enough if there is not too much" (French).[2] Beaumarchais makes Figaro, in speaking of love, to utter the charming hyperbole which has passed into a proverb, "Too much is not enough."[3] Even without being in love, everybody must agree with Voltaire in considering

"Le superflu, chose très nécessaire."

---

[1] Assai è rico a chi non manca.
[2] Assez n'y a, si trop n'y a.
[3] Trop n'est pas assez.

> Better leave than lack.
>
> All covet, all lose.
>
> Covetousness brings nothing home.

"It bursts the bag" (Italian).[1]   Like the dog in the fable, it grasps at the shadow, and lets fall the substance. "He that embraces too much holds nothing fast" (Italian, French).[2]   A statue was erected to Buffon in his lifetime, with the inscription, *Naturam amplectitur omnem* ("He embraces all nature").   Somebody remarked upon this, "He that embraces too much," etc.   Buffon heard of the sarcasm, and had the inscription obliterated.

> It is hard for a greedy eye to hae a leal heart. — *Scotch.*

Covetousness is scarcely consistent with honesty.

> Much would have more.
>
> A greedy eye never had a fu' weam [belly]. — *Scotch.*

"The dust alone can fill the eye of man" (Arab) ; *i. e.* the dust of the grave can alone extinguish the lust of the eye and the cupidity of man.   Among the Arabs, the phrase, "His eye is full," signifies he possesses every object of his desire.   The Germans say, "Greed and the eye can no man fill."[3]   The Scotch say of a covetous person, —

> He 'll get enough ae day when his mouth's fu' o' mools [mould].
>
> The greedy man and the gileynoar [cheat] are soon agreed. — *Scotch.*

---

[1] La codicia rompe il saco.

[2] Chi troppo abbraccia, nulla stringe.   Qui trop embrasse, mal étreint.

[3] Den Geiz und die Augen kann niemand füllen.

"The sharper soon cheats the covetous man" (Spanish).[1]

The grace of God is gear enough. — *Scotch.*

This is the northern form of the proverb which Launcelot Gobbo speaks of as being well parted between Bassanio and Shylock. "You [Bassanio] have the grace of God, and he [Shylock] has enough."

Too much is stark nought. — *Welsh.*
Too much of one thing is good for nothing.

"One may be surfeited with eating tarts" (French).[2] "Nothing too much!" (Latin).[3]

Better a wee fire to warm us than a meikle fire to burn us. — *Scotch.*

It is better to be content with a moderate fortune than attempt to increase it at the risk of being ruined. "Give me the ass that carries me, rather than the horse that throws me" (Portuguese).[4]

Little sticks kindle a fire, but great ones put it out.
Fair and softly goes far in a day.
Hooly and fairly men ride far journeys. — *Scotch.*

"Who goes softly goes safely, and who goes safely goes far" (Italian).[5] "Take-it-easy and Live-long are brothers" (German).[6]

Fools' haste is no speed.

---

[1] El tramposo presto engaña al codicioso.
[2] On se saoule bien de manger tartes.
[3] Ne quid nimis.
[4] Mais quero asno que me leve que cavallo que me derrube.
[5] Chi va piano, va sano, e chi va sano, va lontano.
[6] Gehgemach und Lebelang sind Bruder.

The more haste the worse speed.

This seems to be derived from the Latin adage, *Festinatio tarda est* ("Haste is slow"). It defeats its own purpose by the blunders and imperfect work it occasions. A favorite saying of the Emperors Augustus and Titus was, *Festina lente* ("Hasten leisurely"), which Erasmus calls the king of adages. The Germans have happily translated it,[1] and it is well paraphrased in that saying of Sir Amyas Paulet, "Tarry a little, that we may make an end the sooner." A thing is done "Fast enough if well enough" (Latin).[2]

> Naething in haste but gripping o' fleas. — *Scotch.*
>
> Nothing should be done in haste except catching fleas.
>
> Haste trips up its own heels.

"He that goes too hastily along often stumbles on a fair road" (French).[3] "Reason lies between the bridle and the spur" (Italian).[4]

Draw not your bow till your arrow is fixed.

He that rides ere he be ready wants some o' his graith. — *Scotch.*

He leaves some of his accoutrements behind him. Perhaps one reason why "It is good to have a hatch before your door" is, that it may act as a check upon such unprofitable haste. Sydney Smith adopted a simi-

---

[1] Eile mit Weile.

[2] Sat cito si sat bene.

[3] Qui trop se hâte en cheminant, en beau chemin se fourvoye souvent.

[4] Trà la briglia e lo speron consiste la raggion.

lar expedient, which he called a *screaming gate.* " We all arrived once," he said, " at a friend's house just before dinner, hot, tired, and dusty — a large party assembled — and found all the keys of our trunks had been left behind. Since then I have established a screaming gate. We never set out on our journey now without stopping at a gate about ten minutes' distance from the house, to consider what we have left behind. The result has been excellent."

Two hungry meals make the third a glutton.

Excess in one direction induces excess in the opposite direction.

Soft fire makes sweet malt.

More flies are caught with a drop of honey than with a tun of vinegar.

" Gentleness does more than violence " (French).[1] " The gentle calf sucks all the cows " (Portuguese).[2]

Ower hot, ower cauld. — *Scotch.*

" It may be a fire — on the morrow it will be ashes " (Arab). Violent passions are apt to subside quickly. " Soon fire, soon ashes " (Dutch).

A man may love his house weel, and no ride on the riggin [roof] o 't.
                                                    — *Scotch.*

No one will believe that he loves it the more for any such extravagant demonstration.

---

1 Plus fait douceur que violence.
2 Bezerrinha mansa todas as vaccas mamma.

Many irons in the fire, some will cool.

Too many cooks spoil the broth.

Ower mony greeves [overseers] hinder the wark. — *Scotch.*

"Too many tirewomen make the bride ill dressed" (Spanish).[1] "If the sailors become too numerous the ship sinks" (Arab).

A bow o'erbent will weaken.

All work and no play makes Jack a dull boy.

"This nation, the northern part of it especially, is given to believe in the sovereign efficacy of dulness. To be sure, dulness and solid vice are apt to go hand in hand. But then, according to our notions, dulness is in itself so good a thing — almost a religion. Now, if ever a people required to be amused, it is we sad-hearted Anglo-Saxons. Heavy eaters, hard thinkers, often given up to a peculiar melancholy of our own, with a climate that for months together would frown away mirth if it could, — many of us with very gloomy thoughts about our hereafter. If ever there were a people who should avoid increasing their dulness by all work and no play, we are that people. 'They took their pleasure sadly,' says Froissart, 'after their fashion.' We need not ask of what nation Froissart was speaking." — (*Friends in Council.*)

The mill that is always grinding grinds coarse and fine together.
— *Irish.*

"The pot that boils too much loses flavor" (Portuguese).[2]

---

[1] Muchos componedores descomponen la novia.

[2] Panella que muito ferve, o sabor perde.

Play 's gude while it is play. — *Scotch.*

Beware of pushing it to that point at which it ceases to be play. " Leave off the play (or jest) when it is merriest " (Spanish).[1]   Never let it degenerate into horse play.   " Manual play is clowns' play " (French).[2]

A man may make his own dog bite him.

It is not wise to overstrain authority, or to drive even the weakest or most submissive to desperation.

> **A baited cat may grow as fierce as a lion.**
> **Put a coward on his mettle and he 'll fight the devil.**
> **Make a bridge of gold for the flying enemy.**
> **Extremes meet.**

A proverb of universal application in the physical as well as the moral world.   Every one knows the saying of Napoleon, " From the sublime to the ridiculous is but a step."

> **Too far east is west.**
> **No feast to a miser's.**

---

[1] A la burla, dejarla quando mas agrada.

[2] Jeu de mains, jeu de vilains.

THOROUGH-GOING. — THE WHOLE HOG.

In for a penny, in for a pound.
As good be hanged for a sheep as a lamb.
Ne'er go to the deil wi' a dishclout in your hand. — *Scotch.*
Over shoes, over boots.

"There is nothing like being bespattered for making one defy the slough" (French).[1] These proverbs are as true in their physical as in their moral application. Persons who have ventured a little way will venture further. Persons whose characters are already sullied will not be very careful to preserve them from further discredit. When Madame de Cornuel remonstrated with a court lady on certain improprieties of conduct, the latter exclaimed, "Eh! madame, laissez-moi jouir de ma mauvaise réputation" ("Do let me enjoy the benefit of my bad reputation"). "It is the first shower that wets" (Italian).[2] "It is all the same whether a man has both legs in the stocks or one" (German).[3] Honest Launce "would have one that would be a dog indeed, to be, as it were, a dog in all things." The author of *The Romany Rye* learned a practical illustra-

---

[1] Il n'est que d'être crotté pour affronter le bourbier.
[2] La primiera pioggia è quel che bagna.
[3] Mit beiden Beinen im Stock, oder mit Einem, ist gleichviel.

6

tion of this whole-hog doctrine from an old ostler who had served in his youth at a small inn at Hounslow, much patronized by highwaymen.

" He said that when a person had once made up his mind to become a highwayman, his best policy was to go the whole hog, fearing nothing, but making everybody afraid of him; that people never thought of resisting a savage-faced, foul-mouthed highwayman, and if he were taken were afraid to bear witness against him, lest he should get off and cut their throats some time or other upon the roads; whereas people would resist being robbed by a sneaking, pale-visaged rascal, and would swear bodily against him on the first opportunity; adding that Abershaw and Ferguson, two most awful fellows, had enjoyed a long career, whereas two disbanded officers of the army, who wished to rob a coach like gentlemen, had begged the passengers' pardon, and talked of hard necessity, had been set upon by the passengers themselves, amongst whom were three women, pulled from their horses, conducted to Maidstone, and hanged with as little pity as such contemptible fellows deserved."

Neck or nothing, for the king loves no cripples.

Either break your neck or come off safe: broken limbs will make you a less profitable subject.

Either a man or a mouse.

Either succeed or fail outright. *Aut Cæsar, aut nullus.*

Either win the horse or lose the saddle.

Either make a spoon or spoil a horn.

He that takes the devil into his boat must carry him over the sound.

He that is embarked with the devil must make the passage along with him.

" He that is at sea must either sail or sink " (Danish).
" He that is at sea has not the wind in his hands " (Dutch).[1]

Such things must be if we sell ale.

This was the good woman's reply to her husband when he complained of the exciseman's too demonstrative gallantry.

If you would have the hen's egg you must bear with her cackling.

The cat loves fish, but she is loath to wet her feet.

It is to this proverb that Lady Macbeth alludes when she upbraids her husband for his irresolution :

" Letting ' I dare not ' wait upon ' I would,'
Like the poor cat in the adage."

" There 's no catching trouts with dry breeches " (Portuguese).[2]

Almost and hardly save many a lie.

" Perhaps hinders folk from lying " (French).[3]

Almost was never hanged.

" All but saves many a man " (Danish).[4] " Almost

---

[1] Die op de zee is heeft de wind niet in zijn handen.
[2] Naõ se tomaõ trutas a bragas enxutas.
[3] Peut-être empêche les gens de mentir.
[4] Nær hielper mangen Mand.

kills no man" (Danish).[1] "Almost never killed a fly"
(German) ;[2] for

An inch of a miss is as good as a mile.

This is the original reading of the proverb, and better
than that which is now more current: "A miss is as
good as a mile." The French say, "For a point Martin
lost his ass,"[3] and thereby hangs a tail. An ecclesiastic
named Martin, Abbot of Asello, in Italy, wished to have
this Latin line inscribed over the gate of the abbey:

PORTA PATENS ESTO. NULLI CLAUDARIS HONESTO.

"Gate be open. Never be closed against an honest man."

It was just the time when the long-forgotten art of
punctuation was beginning to be brought into use again.
Abbot Martin was not skilled in this art, and unfortunately he employed a copyist to whom it was equally
unknown. The consequence was, that the point which
ought to have followed the word *esto* was placed after
nulli, completely changing the meaning of the line, thus:

PORTA PATENS ESTO NULLI. CLAUDARIS HONESTO.

"Gate be open never. Be closed against an honest man."

The pope, being informed of this unseemly inscription,
deposed Abbot Martin, and gave the abbey to another.
The new dignitary corrected the punctuation of the
unlucky line, and added the following one:

UNO PRO PUNCTO CARUIT MARTINUS ASELLO.

That is to say, "For a single point Martin lost his

---

[1] Nærved slaaer ingen Mand ihiel.
[2] Beinahe bringt keine Mücke um.
[3] Pour un point Martin perdit son âne.

Asello." But *Asello*, the name of the abbey, being Latin for *ass*, it happened, in the most natural way in the world, that the line was translated thus: "For a point Martin lost his ass," and this erroneous version passed into a proverb. Other accounts of its origin have been given; but that which we have here set down is confirmed by the fact that in Italy they have also another reading of the proverb, namely, *Per un punto Martino perse la cappa* ("For a point Martin lost the cope"); that is, the dignity of abbot typified in that vestment.

WILL. — INCLINATION. — DESIRE.

Where there 's a will there 's a way.
A wight man ne'er wanted a weapon. — *Scotch.*

"A good knight is not at a loss for a lance" (Italian).[1] A man of sense and resolution will make instruments of whatever comes to his hands; and truly "He is not a good mason who refuses any stone" (Italian).[2] "He that has a good head does not want for hats" (French).[3]

Where the will is ready the feet are light.[4]

"The willing dancer is easily played to" (Servian).[5] "The will does it" (German).[6] "A voluntary burden is no burden" (Italian).[7]

"The labor we delight in physics pain."

"A joyous heart spins the hemp" (Servian); and, as Autolycus sings, —

"A merry heart goes all the day,
Your sad tires in a mile-a."

---

[1] A buon cavalier non manca lancia.
[2] Non è buon murator chi rifiuta pietra alcuna.
[3] Qui a bonne tête ne manque pas de chapeaux.
[4] In German, Willig Herz macht leichte Füsse.
[5] Also Flemish, Het is licht genoech ghepepen die gheein danst.
[6] Der Wille thut's.
[7] Carica volontaria non carica.

One man may lead the horse to the water, but fifty can't make him drink.

"You cannot make an ass drink if he is not thirsty" (French).[1] "It is bad coursing with unwilling hounds" (Dutch).[2] "A thing done perforce is not worth a rush" (Italian).[3]

None so deaf as he that will not hear.
Nothing is impossible to a willing mind.

"Madame," said M. de Calonne to a lady who solicited his aid in a certain affair, "if the thing is possible, it is done; and if it is impossible, it shall be done."[4]

Good-will should be taken in part payment.
Take the will for the deed.

"Gifts are as the givers" (German).[5] "The will gives the work its name." "The will is the soul of the work" (German).[6]

Hell is paved with good intentions.

A great moral conveyed in a bold figure. What is the worth of virtuous resolutions that never ripen into action? In the German version of the proverb a slight change greatly improves the metaphor, thus: "The

---

[1] On ne saurait faire boire un âne s'il n'a pas soif.

[2] Med onwillige honden is kwaad hazen vangen.

[3] Cosa fatta per forza non val una scorza.

[4] Madame, si la chose est possible, elle est dejà faite; et si elle est impossible, elle se fera.

[5] Die Gaben sind wie die Geber.

[6] Der Wille giebt dem Werke den Namen. Der Wille ist des Werkes Seele.

way to perdition is paved with good intentions."[1] A
Scotch proverb warns the weak in will, who are always
hoping to reform and do well, that

Hopers go to hell.

As the fool thinks, the bell tinks.

We are all prone to interpret facts and tokens in
accordance with our own inclinations and habits of
thought. It was not the voice of the bells that first
inspired young Whittington with hopes of attaining
civic honors; it was because he had conceived such hopes
already that he was able to hear so distinctly the words,
"Turn again, Whittington, thrice Lord Mayor of London." "People make the bells say whatever they
have a mind" (French).[2] In a Latin sermon on wid-
owhood by Jean Raulin, a monk of Cluny of the
fifteenth century, there is a story which Rabelais has
told again in his own way. Raulin's version is this:
A widow consulted her parish priest about her
entering into a second marriage. She told him she
stood in need of a helpmate and protector, and that her
journeyman, for whom she had taken a fancy, was in-
dustrious and well acquainted with her late husband's
trade. "Very well," said the priest, "you had better
marry him." "And yet," rejoined the widow, "I am
afraid to do it, for who knows but I may find my servant become my master?" "Well, then," said the
priest, "don't have him." "But what shall I do?" said

---

[1] Der Weg zum Verderben est mit guten Vorsätzen gepflastert.
[2] On fait dire aux cloches tout ce qu'on veut.

the widow;"the business left me by my poor dear departed husband is more than I can manage by myself." "Marry him, then," said the priest. "Ay, but suppose he turns out a scamp," said the widow; "he may get hold of my property, and run through it all." "Don't have him," said the priest. Thus the dialogue went on, the priest always agreeing in the last opinion expressed by the widow, until at length, seeing that her mind was actually made up to marry the journeyman, he told her to consult the church bells, and they would advise her best what to do. The bells were rung, and the widow heard them distinctly say, "Do take your man; do take your man."[1] Accordingly she went home and married him forthwith; but it was not long before he thrashed her soundly, and made her feel that instead of his mistress she had become his servant. Back she went to the priest, cursing the hour when she had been credulous enough to act upon his advice. "Good woman," said he, "I am afraid you did not rightly understand what the bells said to you." He rang them again, and then the poor woman heard clearly, but too late, these warning words: "Do not take him; do not take him."[2]

> Wilful will do it.
> A wilfu' man maun hae his way. — *Scotch.*
> He that will to Cupar maun to Cupar. — *Scotch.*

Cupar is a town in Fife, and that is all that Scotch paræmiologists condescend to tell us about it. I suppose

---

[1] Prends ton valet; prends ton valet.
[2] Ne le prends pas; ne le prends pas.

there is some special reason why insisting on going to Cupar, above all other towns, is a notable proof of pig-headedness.

A wilful man never wanted woe.

A wilfu' man should be unco' wise. — *Scotch.*

Since he chooses to rely on his own wisdom only.

Forbidden fruit is sweet.

"Sweet is the apple when the keeper is away" (Latin).[1]

> " Stolen sweets are always sweeter ;
> Stolen kisses much completer ;
> Stolen looks are nice in chapels ;
> Stolen, stolen be your apples ! "

So sings Leigh Hunt, translating from the Latin of Thomas Randolph. The doctrine of these poets is as old as Solomon, who says, "Stolen waters are sweet," — a sentence thus paraphrased in German : " Forbidden water is Malmsey."[2] A story is told of a French lady, says Madame du Barry, who happened once, by some extraordinary chance, to have nothing but pure water to drink when very thirsty. She took a deep draught, and finding in it what the Roman emperor had sighed for in vain — a new pleasure — she cried out, "Ah! what a pity it is that drinking water is not a sin!"

"There is no pleasure but palls, and all the more if it costs nothing" (Spanish).[3] "The sweetest grapes hang highest" (German).[4] "The figs on the far side

---

[1] Dulce pomum quum abest custos.

[2] Verbotenes Wasser ist Malvasier.

[3] No hay placer que no enhade, y mas se cuesta de balde.

[4] Die süssessten Trauben hangen am höchsten.

of the hedge are sweeter" (Servian). "Every fish that escapes appears greater than it is" (Turkish). Upon the same principle it is that what nature never intended a man to do is often the very thing he particularly desires to do. "A man who can't sing is always striving to sing" (Latin) ;[1] and generally "He who can't do, always wants to do" (Italian).[2]

Forbid a fool a thing, and that he'll do.

Of course ; and so will many a one who is otherwise no fool. What mortal man, to say nothing of women, but would have done as Bluebeard's wife did when left in the castle with the key of that mysterious chamber in her hand ?

Every man has his hobby.

Some men pay dearly for theirs. "Hobby horses are more costly than Arabians" (German).[3]

You may pay too dear for your whistle.

The origin of this saying, which has become thoroughly proverbial, is found in the following extract from a paper by its author, Benjamin Franklin :—
"When I was a child of seven years old my friends on a holiday filled my pockets with coppers. I went directly to a shop where they sold toys for children, and being charmed with the sound of a whistle that I met by the way in the hands of another boy, I volun-

---

[1] Qui nescit canere semper canere laborat.
[2] Chi non puole, sempre vuole.
[3] Steckenpferde sind theuerer als arabische Hengste.

tarily offered him all my money for it. I then came
home, and went whistling all over the house, much
pleased with my whistle, but disturbing all the family.
My brothers, and sisters, and cousins, understanding the
bargain I had made, told me I had given for it four
times as much as it was worth. This put me in mind
what good things I might have bought with the rest of
the money; and they laughed at me so much for my
folly that I cried with vexation, and the reflection gave
me more chagrin than the whistle gave me pleasure.
This, however, was afterwards of use to me, the im-
pression continuing on my mind; so that often when I
was tempted to buy some unnecessary thing I said to
myself, ' Don't give too much for the whistle;' and so I
saved my money. As I grew up, came into the world,
and observed the actions of men, I met with many, very
many, who gave too much for the whistle."

CUSTOM. — HABIT. — USE.

Use will make a man live in a lion's den.
Custom is second nature.

CICERO says nearly the same thing,[1] and the thought has been happily amplified by Sydney Smith. "There is no degree of disguise or distortion which human nature may not be made to assume from habit; it grows in every direction in which it is trained, and accommodates itself to every circumstance which caprice or design places in its way. It is a plant with such various aptitudes, and such opposite propensities, that it flourishes in a hothouse or the open air; is terrestrial or aquatic, parasitical or independent; looks well in exposed situations, thrives in protected ones; can bear its own luxuriance, admits of amputation; succeeds in perfect liberty, and can be bent down into any forms of art; it is so flexible and ductile, so accommodating and vivacious, that of two methods of managing it — completely opposite — neither the one nor the other need be considered as mistaken and bad. Not that habit can give any new principle; but of those numerous principles which *do* exist in our nature it entirely determines the order and force."[2]

[1] Ferme in naturam consuetudo vestitur. — (*De Invent.* i. 2.)
[2] "Lectures on Moral Philosophy."

Once a use and ever a custom.

"Continuance becomes usage" (Italian).[1] Whatever
we do often we become more and more apt to do, till at
last the propensity to the act becomes irresistible, though
the performance of it may have ceased to give any pleasure. In Fielding's "Life of Jonathan Wild" the great
thief is represented as playing at cards with the Count,
a professed gambler. "Such was the power of habit
over the minds of these illustrious persons, that Mr.
Wild could not keep his hands out of the Count's
pockets, though he knew they were empty; nor could
the Count abstain from palming a card, though he was
well aware Mr. Wild had no money to pay him." "To
change a habit is like death" (Spanish).[2]

Hand in use is father o' lear [learning, skill]. — Scotch.
Practice makes perfect.

"By working in the smithy one becomes a smith"
(Latin, French).[3] "Use makes the craftsman" (Spanish, German).[4] An emir had bought a left eye of a
glassmaker, and was vexed at finding that he could not
see with it. The man begged him to give it a little
time; he could not expect that it would see all at once
as well as the right eye, which had been for so many
years in the habit of it. We take this whimsical story
from Coleridge, who does not tell us in what Oriental
Joe Miller he found it.

---

[1] Continuanza diventa usanza.
[2] Mudar costumbre a par de muerte.
[3] Fabricando fit faber. En forgeant on devient forgeron.
[4] El usar saca oficial. Uebung macht den Meister.

No man is his craft's master the first day.

But some people fancy themselves masters born, like "The Portuguese apprentice, who does not know how to sew, and wants to cut out" (Spanish).[1]

You must spoil before you spin.

"One learns by failing" (French).[2] "He that stumbles, if he does not fall, quickens his pace" (Spanish).[3]

Eith to learn the cat to the kirn. — *Scotch.*

That is, it is easy to teach the cat the way to the churn. Bad habits are easily acquired.

A bad custom is like a good cake — better broken than kept.

On this proverb is built, perhaps, that remark of Hamlet's which has troubled some hypercritical commentators, "A custom more honored in the breach than in the observance." An energetic Spanish proverb counsels us to "Break the leg of a bad habit."[4]

At Rome do as Rome does.

"Wherever you be, do as you see" (Spanish).[5] A very terse German proverb, which can only be paraphrased in English, signifies that whatever is customary in any country is proper and becoming there; or, as we might say, "After the land's manner is mannerly."[6]

---

[1] Aprendiz de Portugal, no sabe cozer y quiere cortar.
[2] On apprend en faillant.
[3] Quien estropieca, si no cae, el camino adelanta.
[4] A mal costumbre, quebrarle la pierna.
[5] Por donde fueres, haz como vieres.
[6] Ländlich, sittlich.

The Livonians say, "In the land of the naked, people are ashamed of clothes." "So many countries, so many customs" (French).[1] In a Palais Royal farce a captain's wife is deploring her husband, who has been eaten by the Caffres. Her servant observes, by way of consolation, *Mais, madame, que voulez-vous? Chaque peuple a ses usages* ("Well, well, ma'am, after all, every people has its own manners and customs").

Tell me the company you keep, and I'll tell you what you are.
Tell me with whom thou goest, and I'll tell thee what thou doest.

"He that lives with cripples learns to limp" (Dutch).[2] "He that goes with wolves learns to howl" (Spanish) ;[3] and "He that lies down with dogs gets up with fleas" (Spanish.)[4]

As good be out of the world as out of the fashion.

Mrs. Hutchinson tells us that, although her husband acted with the Puritan party, they would not allow him to be religious because his hair was not in their cut. The world will more readily forgive a breach of all the Ten Commandments than a violation of one of its own conventional rules. "Fools invent fashions, and wise men follow them" (French).[5] "Better be mad with all the world than wise alone" (French).[6]

---

1 Tant de pays, tant de guises.
2 Die bij kreupelen woont, leert hinken.
3 Quien con lobos anda, á aullar se enseña.
4 Quien con perros se echa, con pulgas se levanta.
5 Les fous inventent les modes, et les sages les suivent.
6 Il vaut mieux être fou avec tous que sage tout seul.

The used key is always bright.

" 'If I rest, I rust,' it says " (German).[1]

but

Drawn wells have sweetest water;

Standing pools gather filth.

Drawn wells are seldom dry.

---

[1] Rast ich, so rost ich, sagt der Schlüssel.

7

SELF-CONCEIT. — SPURIOUS PRETENSIONS.

How we apples swim!

So said the horsedung as it floated down the stream along with fruit.

"We hounds slew the hare," quoth the messan [lapdog]. — *Scotch.*

"They came to shoe the horses of the pacha; the beetle then stretched out its leg" (Arab). We read in the Talmud that "All kinds of wood burn silently except thorns, which crackle and call out, 'We, too, are wood.'" "It was prettily devised of Æsop," says Lord Bacon : "the fly sat upon the axle of the chariot, and said, 'What a dust do I raise!'"

A' Stuarts are no sib to the king. — *Scotch.*

That is, not all who bear that name belong to the royal race of Stuarts. "There are fagots and fagots,"[1] as Molière says. "It is some way from Peter to Peter" (Spanish).[2] Great is the difference between the terrible lion of the Atlas and the Cape lion, the most currish of

---

[1] Il y a fagots et fagots.
[2] Algo va de Pedro a Pedro.

enemies; but the distinction is not always borne in mind by the readers of hunting adventures in Africa. The traditional name of lion beguiles the imagination of the unwary. In like manner some people think that

"A book's a book, although there's nothing in it."

Every ass thinks himself worthy to stand with the king's horses.

But asses deceive themselves. "He that is a donkey, and believes himself a deer, finds out his mistake at the leaping of the ditch" (Italian).[1] "Doctor Luther's shoes will not fit every village priest" (German).[2]

Many talk of Robin Hood that never shot in his bow.

Like Justice Shallow, who "talks," says Falstaff, "as familiarly of John of Gaunt as if he had been sworn brother to him; and I'll be sworn he never saw him but once in the tilt-yard, and then he burst his head for crowding among the marshal's men." Southey, in his "Omniana," has applied this proverb to that numerous class of literary pretenders who quote and criticise flippantly works known to them only at secondhand. A conspicuous living example of this class is M. Ponsard, who, on the occasion of his reception into the French Academy, discoursed about Shakspeare, and talked of him as "the divine WILLIAMS," by way of evincing his proficiency in the language of the great dramatist whose works he disparaged.

---

[1] Chi asino é, e cervo si crede, al salto del fosso se ne avvede.

[2] Doctor Luthers Schuhe sind nicht allen Dorfpriestern gerecht.

The man on the dyke is always the best hurler. — *Munster.*

The looker-on is quite sure he could do better than the actual players. In Connaught, which is as renowned for its neck-or-nothing riders as Munster is for its vigorous hurlers, they have this parallel saying, —

The best horseman is always on his feet.

In the same sense the Dutch aver that "The best pilots stand on shore."[1]

In a calm sea every man is a pilot.
Every man can tame a shrew but he that hath her.
Bachelors' wives and maids' children are always well taught.

"He that has no wife chastises her well; he that has no children rears them well" (Italian).[2]

I ask your pardon, coach; I thought you were a wheelbarrow when I stumbled over you. — *Irish.*

An ironical apology for offence given to overweening vanity or pride.

The pride of the cobbler's dog, that took the wall of a wagon of hay, and was squeezed to death.

---

[1] De beste stuurlieden staan aan land.

[2] Chi non ha moglie, ben la batte ; chi non ha figliuoli, ben gli pasce.

SELF-LOVE.—SELF-INTEREST.— SELF-RELIANCE.

Charity begins at home.

THIS is literally true in the most exalted sense. The best of men are those

> " Whose circling charities begin
> With the few loved ones Heaven has placed them near,
> Nor cease till all mankind are in their sphere."

It is only in irony, or by an odious abuse of its meaning, that the proverb is ever used as an apology for that sort of charity which not only begins at home, but ends there likewise. The egotist holds that "Self is the first object of charity" (Latin).[1] "Every one has his hands turned towards himself" (Polish).

The priest christens his own child first.
Every man draws the water to his own mill.

"Every cow licks her own calf." "Every old woman blows under her own kettle" (both Servian). "Every one rakes the embers to his own cake" (Arab).

Every one for himself, and God for us all.
Let every tub stand on its own bottom.

---

[1] Prima sibi charitas.

Let every sheep hang by its own shank.
Let every herring hang by its own gills.
Ilka man for his ain hand, as John Jelly fought. — *Scotch.*

James Kelly gives this explanation of the last proverb : " As two men were fighting, John Jelly, going by, made up fiercely to them. Each of them asked him which he was for ; he answered, for his own hand, and beat them both." Sir Walter Scott puts aside John Jelly's claims to the authorship of this saying, and assigns it to Harry Smith in the following passage of " The Fair Maid of Perth." After the fight between the clans at the North Inch, Black Douglas says to the smith, —

" ' If thou wilt follow me, good fellow, I will change thy leathern apron for a knight's girdle, thy burgage tenement for an hundred-pound-land to maintain thy rank withal.'

" ' I thank you humbly, my lord,' said the smith dejectedly, ' but I have shed blood enough already ; and Heaven has punished me by foiling the only purpose for which I entered the contest.'

" ' How, friend ? ' said Douglas. ' Didst thou not fight for the Clan Chattan, and have they not gained a glorious conquest ? '

" ' I fought for my own hand,' said the smith indifferently ; and the expression is still proverbial in Scotland, meaning, ' I did such a thing for my own pleasure, not for your profit.' "

Let every man skin his own skunk. — *American.*

The skunk stinks ten thousand times worse than a polecat. " Let every one carry his own sack to the mill" (German).[1] "Let every fox take care of his own tail" (Italian).[2]

Self do, self have.

Analogous to this manly proverb, as it seems to me, is that Dutch one, "Self's the man,"[3] which Dean Trench has stigmatized as merely selfish.

The tod [fox] ne'er sped better than when he went his ain errand. — *Scotch.*

The miller ne'er got better moulter [toll] than he took wi' his ain hands. — *Scotch.*

If you would have your business done, go; if not, send.

If you would have a thing well done, do it yourself.

Ilka man's man had a man, and that made the Treve fa'.— *Scotch.*

The Treve was a strong castle built by Black Douglas. The governor left the care of it to a deputy, and he to an under-deputy, through whose negligence the castle was taken and burned. "The master bids the man, and the man bids the cat, and the cat bids its tail" (Portuguese).[4] General Sir Charles Napier, speaking of what happened during his temporary absence from the government of Corfu, says, "How entirely all things depend on the mode of executing them, and how ridiculous mere theories are! My successor thought, as half the world always thinks, that a man in command has only to order, and obedience will follow. Hence they are baffled, not from want of talent,

---

[1] Trage Jeder seinem Sack zur Mülle.

[2] Ogni volpe habbia cura della sua coda.

[3] Zelf is de Man.

[4] Manda o amo ao moço, o moço ao gato, e o gato ao rabo.

but from inactivity, vainly thinking that while they spare themselves every one under them will work like horses."

Trust not to another for what you can do yourself.

" Let him that has a mouth not say to another, Blow " (Spanish).[1]

The master's eye will do more work than both his hands.

" If you have money to throw away, set on workmen and don't stand by " (Italian) ;[2] for

> When the cat's away the mice will play.
> The eye of the master fattens the steed.
> The master's eye puts mate on the horse's bones. —*Ulster.*

" The answers of Perses and Libys are worth observing," says Aristotle. " The former being asked what was the best thing to make a horse fat, answered, ' The master's eye ;' the other being asked what was the best manure, answered, ' The master's footsteps.' " The Spaniards have naturalized this last saying among them.[3] Aulus Gellius tells a story of a man who, being asked why he was so fat, and the horse he rode was so lean, replied, " Because I feed myself, and my servant feeds my horse."

> He that owns the cow goes nearest her tail. —*Scotch.*
> Let him that owns the cow take her by the tail.

In some districts formerly the cattle used to suffer

---

[1] Quien tiene boca no diga á otro, sopla.

[2] Chi ha quattrini a buttar via, metti operaji, e non vi stia.

[3] El pie del dueño estiercol para la heredad.

greatly from want of food in winter and the early months of spring, before the grass had begun to grow. Sometimes a cow would become so weak from inanition as to be unable to rise if she once lay down. In that case it was necessary to lift her up by means of ropes passed under her, and, above all, by pulling at her tail. This part of the job being the most important, was naturally undertaken by the owner of the animal.

> A man is a lion in his own cause.
> No man cries stinking fish.

On the contrary, every man tries to set off his wares to the best advantage, to make the most of his own case, etc. "Every one says, 'I have right on my side'" (French).[1] Æsop's currier maintained that for fortifying a town there was "nothing like leather." "Every potter praises his pot, and all the more if it is cracked" (Spanish).[2] "'T is a mad priest who blasphemes his relics" (Italian).[3] "Ask the host if he has good wine" (Italian).[4] One canny Scot compliments another with the remark, —

> Ye'll no sell your hens on a rainy day;

for then the drenched feathers, sticking close to the skin, give the poor things a lean and miserable appearance.

> It is an ill bird that fouls its own nest.
> He was scant o' news that tauld his feyther was hangit. — *Scotch.*

---

[1] Chacun dit, "J'ai bon droit."
[2] Cada ollero su olla alaba, y mas el que la tiene quebrada.
[3] Matto è quel prete chi bestemma le sue reliquie.
[4] Dimanda al hosto s'egli ha buon vino.

They 're scarce of news that speak ill of their mother. —*Ulster.*

Why wantonly proclaim one's own disgrace, or expose
the faults or weaknesses of one's kindred or people?
"If you have lost your nose, put your hand before the
place" (Italian).[1] Napoleon I. used to say, "People
should wash their foul linen in private." It is a necessary process, but there is no need to obtrude it on public
notice. English writers often quote this maxim of the
great emperor, but always mistranslate it. *Il faut laver
son linge sale en famille* is one of those idiomatic phrases
which cannot be perfectly rendered in another tongue.
Our version of it comes near to its meaning, which is
quite lost in that which is commonly given, "People
should wash their foul linen at home." The point of
the proverb lies in the privacy it enjoins, and this might
equally be secured whether the linen was washed at
home or sent away to the laundress's. *En famille* and
at home are not mutually equivalent; the former means
more than the latter. We may say of a man who en-
tertains a large dinner party in his own house, that he
dines at home, but not that he dines *en famille.*

No one knows where the shoe pinches so well as he that wears it.
I wot weel where my ain shoe binds me. — *Scotch.*

Erskine used to say that when the hour came that all
secrets should be revealed we should know the reason
why — shoes are always too tight. The authorship of
this proverb is commonly ascribed to Æmilius Paulus;
but the story told by Plutarch leaves it doubtful whether

---

[1] Se tu hai meno il naso, ponviti una mano.

Æmilius used a known illustration or invented one. The relations of his wife remonstrated with him on his determination to repudiate her, she being an honorable matron, against whom no fault could be alleged. Æmilius admitted the lady's worth; but, pointing to one of his shoes, he asked the remonstrants what they thought of it. They thought it a handsome, well-fitting shoe. "But none of you," he rejoined, "can tell where it pinches me."

The heart knoweth its own bitterness. — *Solomon.*

"To every one his own cross seems heaviest" (Italian);[1] but "The burden is light on the shoulders of another" (Russian); and "One does not feel three hundred blows on another's back" (Servian). "Another's care hangs by a hair" (Spanish).[2] "Another's woe is a dream" (French).[3] Rochefoucauld has had the credit of saying, "We all have fortitude enough to endure the woes of others;" but it is plain from this and other examples that he was not the sole author of "Rochefoucauld's Maxims."

"The case is altered," quoth Plowden.

Edmund Plowden, an eminent lawyer in Queen Elizabeth's time, was asked by a neighbor what remedy there was in law against the owner of some hogs that had trespassed on the inquirer's ground. Plowden an-

---

[1] Ad ognuno par più grave la croce sua.

[2] Cuidado ageno de pelo cuelga.

[3] Mal d'autrui n'est que songe.

swered, he might have a very good remedy. "Marry, then," said the other, "the hogs are your own." "Nay, then, neighbor, the case is altered," quoth Plowden. Others, says Ray, with more probability make this the original of the proverb: "Plowden being a Roman Catholic, some neighbors of his who bare him no good-will, intending to entrap him and bring him under the lash of the law, had taken care to dress up an altar in a certain place, and provided a layman in a priest's habit, who should say mass there at such a time. And, withal, notice thereof was given privately to Mr. Plowden, who thereupon went and was present at the mass. For this he was presently accused and indicted. He at first stands upon his defence, and would not acknowledge the thing. Witnesses are produced, and among the rest one who deposed that he himself performed the mass, and saw Mr. Plowden there. Saith Plowden to him, 'Art thou a priest, then?' The fellow replied, 'No.' 'Why, then, gentlemen, quoth he, 'the case is altered; no priest, no mass,' which came to be a proverb, and continues still in Shropshire with this addition. 'The case is altered,' quoth Plowden: 'no priest, no mass.'"

That's Hackerton's cow.

This is a proverb of the Scotch, and they tell a story about it similar to the first of the two above related of Plowden. Hackerton was a lawyer, whose cow had gored a neighbor's ox. The man told him the reverse. "Why, then," said Hackerton, "your ox must go for my heifer — the law provides that." "No," said the man, your cow killed my ox." "The case alters there," said

Hackerton. Many a one exclaims in secret with the Spaniard, "Justice, but not brought home to myself"![1] "Nobody likes that" (Italian).[2]

> Close sits my shirt, but closer my skin.

That is, I love my friends well, but myself better; or, my body is dearer to me than my goods.

> Near is my petticoat, but nearer is my smock.

Some friends are nearer to me than others. There are many proverbs in various languages similar to the last two in meaning and in form, but with different terms of comparison. They are all modelled upon the Latin adage, "The tunic is nearer than the frock."[3]

---

[1] Justicia, mas no por mi casa.
[2] A nessuno piace la giustizia a casa sua.
[3] Tunica pallio propior.

SELFISHNESS IN GIVING.—SPURIOUS BENEVOLENCE.

Throw in a sprat to catch a salmon.

To give an apple where there is an orchard.

The hen's egg aft gaes to the ha'
To bring the guse's egg awa'. — *Scotch.*

"He gives an egg to get a chicken" (Dutch).[1] "Giving is fishing" (Italian).[2] "To one who has a pie in the oven you may give a bit of your cake" (French).[3]

Have a horse of thine own, and thou may'st borrow another's.
— *Welsh.*

"People don't give black-puddings to one who kills no pigs" (Spanish).[4] In Spain it is usual, when a pig is killed at home, to make black-puddings, and give some of them to one's neighbors. There is thrift in this; for black-puddings will not keep long in that climate, and each man generally makes more than enough for his own consumption. "People lend only to the

---

[1] Hij geeft een ei, om een kucken te krijgen.
[2] Donare si chiama pescare.
[3] A celui qui a son pâté au four, on peut donner de son gateau.
[4] A quien no mata puerco, no le dan morcilla.

rich" (French).[1] "People give to the rich, and take from the poor" (German).[2] "He that eats capon gets capon" (French).[3]

He that has a goose will get a goose.

When the child is christened you may have godfathers enough.

Offers of service abound when a man no longer needs them. "When our daughter is married sons-in-law turn up" (Spanish).[4]

When I am dead make me caudle.

When Tom's pitcher is broken I shall get the sherds.

Tom's generosity is like the charity of the Abbot of Bamba, who "Gives away for the good of his soul what he can't eat" (Spanish).[5] The dying bequest of another worthy of the same nation is proverbial. One of his cows had strayed away and been long missing. His last orders were, that if this cow were found it should be for his children; if otherwise, it should be for God. Hence the proverb, "Let that which is lost be for God."

They are free of fruit that want an orchard.

They are aye gudewilly o' their horse that hae nane. — *Scotch.*

Their good-natured willingness to lend it is remarkable. "No one is so open-handed as he who has nothing

---

[1] On ne prête qu'aux riches.

[2] Reichen giebt man, Armen nimmt man.

[3] Qui chapon mange, chapon lui vient.

[4] A hija casada salen nos yernos.

[5] El abad de Bamba, lo que no puede comer, da lo por su alma.

to give" (French).[1]   "He that cannot is always willing" (Italian).[2]

Hens are free o' horse corn. — *Scotch.*

People are apt to be very liberal of what does not
belong to them.   "Broad thongs are cut from other
men's leather" (Latin).[3]   "Of my gossip's loaf a large
slice for my godson" (Spanish).[4]

Steal the goose, and give the giblets in alms.

"Steal the pig, and give away the pettitoes for God's
sake" (Spanish).[5]

---

[1] Nul n'est si large que celui qui n'a rien à donner.

[2] Chi non puole, sempre vuole.

[3] Ex alieno tergore lata secantur lora.

[4] Del pan de mi compadre buen zatico á mi ahijado.

[5] Hurtar el puerco, y dar los pies por Dios.

INGRATITUDE.

Save a thief from the gallows, and he will be the first to cut your throat.

The galley-slaves whom Don Quixote rescued repaid the favor by pelting him and his squire with stones, and stealing Sancho's ass. The French have two parallels for the English proverb. "Take a churl from the gibbet, and he will put you on it;"[1] and, "Unhang one that is hanged, and he will hang thee."[2] Observe the comprehensiveness of this second proposition; it seems to embody an old superstition not yet quite extinct, for it warns us against the danger of rescuing *any* man from the rope, no matter how he may have come to have his neck in the noose. An incident curiously illustrative of this doctrine was thus narrated in a Belgian newspaper, the *Constitutionnel* of Mons, of July 4th, 1856:

"The day before yesterday a man hanged himself at Wasmes. Another man chanced to come upon him before life was extinct, and cut him down in a state of insensibility. Presently up came some women, who clamorously protested against the rashness, not of the would-

---

[1] Otez un vilain du gibet, il vous y mettra.
[2] Dépends le pendard, il te pendra.

be suicide, but of his rescuer, and assured the latter that his only chance of escaping the dangers to which his imprudent humanity exposed him was to hang the poor wretch up again. The man was so alarmed that he was actually proceeding to do as they advised him, when fortunately the burgomaster arrived just in time to prevent that act of barbarous stupidity."

This incident will at once remind the reader of the wreck scene in *The Pirate*. Mordaunt Merton is hastening to save Cleveland, when Bryce Snailsfoot thus remonstrates with him: "Are you mad? You that have lived sae lang in Zetland to risk the saving of a drowning man? Wot ye not, if you bring him to life again, he will be sure to do you some capital injury?"

Put a snake in your bosom, and when it is warm it will sting you.

" Bring up a raven, and it will peck out your eyes " (Spanish, German).[1] " Do good to a knave, and pray God he requite thee not " (Danish).[2]

I taught you to swim, and now you'd drown me.

A's tint that's put into a riven dish. — *Scotch.*

All is lost that is put into a broken dish, or that is bestowed upon a thankless person. The Arabs say, " Eat the present, and break the dish " (in which it was brought). The dish will otherwise remind you of the obligation.

---

[1] Cria el cuervo, y sacarte ha los ojos. Erziehst du dir einen Raben, so wird er dir die Augen ausgraben.

[2] Giör vel imod en Skalk, og bed til Gud han lönner dig ikke.

Eaten bread is soon forgotten.

"A favor to come is better than a hundred received" (Italian).[1] Who was it that first defined gratitude as a lively sense of future favors? "When I confer a favor" said Louis XIV., "I make one ingrate and a hundred malcontents."

---

[1] Val più un piacere da farsi, che cento di quelli fatti.

THE MOTE AND THE BEAM.

Those who live in glass houses should not throw stones.

In Timbs's "Things not Generally Known" it is related that, "In the reign of James I. the Scotch adventurers who came over with that monarch were greatly annoyed by persons breaking the windows of their houses, and among the instigators was Buckingham, the court favorite, who lived in a large house in St. Martin's Fields, which, from the great number of windows, was termed the Glass House. Now the Scotchmen, in retaliation, broke the windows of Buckingham's mansion. The courtier complained to the king, to whom the Scotchmen had previously applied, and the monarch replied to Buckingham, 'Those who live in glass houses, Steenie, should be careful how they throw stones.' *Whence arose the common saying.*"

It did not arise thence, nor was King James its inventor. This is one of a thousand instances in which a story growing out of a proverb has been presented as that proverb's origin. "Let him that has glass tiles [panes] not throw stones at his neighbor's house" is a maxim common to the Spaniards[1] and Italians,[2] and

---

[1] El que tiene tejados de vidrio no tire piedras al de su vicino.
[2] Chi ha tegoli di vetro non tiri sassi al vicino.

older than the time of James I. The Italians say also, " Let him that has a glass skull not take to stone-throwing."[1]

The kiln calls the oven burnt house.

The pot calls the kettle black bottom.

When negroes quarrel they always call each other " dam niggers." " The pan says to the pot, ' Keep off, or you 'll smutch me ' " (Italian).[2] " The shovel makes game of the poker" (French).[3] " Said the raven to the crow, ' Get out of that, blackamoor' " (Spanish).[4] " One ass nicknames another Longears" (German).[5] " Dirty-nosed folk always want to wipe other folks' noses " (French).[6]

"Crooked carlin!" quoth the cripple to his wife. — *Scotch.*

"God help the fool!" said the idiot.

Who more ready to call her neighbor "scold" than the arrantest scold in the parish?

"A harlot repented for one night. ' Is there no police officer,' she exclaimed, ' to take up harlots?' " (Arab.)

Point not at others' spots with a foul finger.

Physician, heal thyself.

"Among wonderful things," say the Arabs of Egypt, is a sore-eyed person who is an oculist."

---

[1] Chi ha testa di vetro non faccia a' sassi.

[2] La padella dice al pajuolo, Fatti in la che tu mi tigni.

[3] La pêle se moque du fourgon.

[4] Dijó la corneja al cuervo, Quitate allá, negro.

[5] Ein Esel schimpft den andern, Langohr.

[6] Les morveux veulent toujours moucher les autres.

FAULTS. — EXCUSES. — UNEASY CONSCIOUSNESS.

Lifeless, faultless.

It is a good horse that never stumbles.

To which some add, "And a good wife that never grumbles." None are immaculate. "Are there not spots on the very sun?" (French).[1] A member of the parliament of Toulouse, apologizing to the king or his minister for the judicial murder of Calas perpetrated by that body, quoted the proverb, "*Il n'y a si bon cheval qui ne bronche*" ("It is a good horse," etc.). He was answered, "*Passe pour un cheval, mais toute l'écurie!*" ("A horse, granted; but the whole stable!")

He that shoots always right forfeits his arrow. — *Welsh*.

But in no instance was the forfeit ever exacted, for the best archer will sometimes miss the mark, just as "The best driver will sometimes upset" (French).[2] "A good fisherman may let an eel slip from him" (French);[3] and "A good swimmer is not safe from all chance of

---

[1] Le soleil lui-même, n'a-t-il pas des taches ?
[2] Il n'est si bon charretier qui ne verse.
[2] A bon pêcheur échappe anguille.

drowning" (French).[1] "The priest errs at the altar"
(Italian).[2]

They ne'er beuk [baked] a gude cake but may bake an ill. — *Scotch.*

He rode sicker [sure] that ne'er fell. — *Scotch.*

It is a sound head that has not a soft piece in it.

Every rose has its prickles.

Every bean has its black.

Every path has its puddle.

There never was a good town but had a mire at one end of it.

" He who wants a mule without fault may go afoot"
(Spanish).[3]

A' things wytes [blames] that no weel fares. — *Scotch.*

When a man fails in what he undertakes he will be
sure to lay the blame on anything or anybody rather
than on himself. " He that does amiss never lacks excuses" (Italian).[4] "He is a bad shot who cannot find
an excuse" (German).[5] "The archer that shoots ill
has a lie ready" (Spanish).[6] That is rather a strong
expression: the Italians, with a more refined apprecia-
tion of the eloquence displayed by missing marksmen,
declare that " A fine shot never killed a bird."[7]

---

1 Bon nageur de n'être noyé n'est pas sûre.

2 Erra il prete all' altare.

3 Quien quisiere mula sin tacha, andese á pie.

4 A chi fa male mai mancano scuse.

5 Ein schlechter Schütz der keine Ausrede findet.

6 Vallestero que mal tira, presto tiene la mentira.

7 Bel colpo non ammazzò mai uccello.

A bad workman always complains of his tools.

A bad excuse is better than none.

This, of course, is ironical. The Italians hold that "Any excuse is good provided it avails" (Italian) ;[1] and, "Any excuse will serve when one has not a mind to do a thing."[2] We may easily guess what the Spaniards mean by "Friday pretexts for not fasting."[3]

"Who can help sickness?" quoth the drunken wife, when she lay in the gutter.

Guilt is jealous.

A guilty conscience needs no accuser.

Touch a galled horse, and he 'll wince.

A galled horse will not endure the comb.

"Let the galled jade wince, our withers are unwrung," cries Hamlet, mockingly, as he reads the effect of the play in the fratricide's countenance. "He that is in fault is [steeped] in suspicion" (Italian),[4] and his uneasy conscience betrays itself at every casual touch. He is like "One who has a straw tail," and "is always afraid of its catching fire" (Italian).[5]

He that has a muckle [big] nose thinks ilka ane is speaking o't.
— Scotch.

"Hair is not to be mentioned in a bald man's house"

---

[1] Ogni scusa è buona, pur che vaglia.

[2] Ogni scusa è buona, quando non si vuol far alcuna cosa.

[3] Achaques al viernes por no le ayunar.

[4] Chi è in difetto, è in sospetto.

[5] Chi ha coda di paglia ha sempre paura che gli pigli fuoco.

(Livonian). "Never speak of a rope in the house of one who was hanged" (Italian);[1] or, as the Hebrew form of the precept runs, "He that hath had one of his family hanged may not say to his neighbor, 'Hang up this fish.'" Formerly the French used to say, "It is not right to speak of a rope *in presence* of one who has been hanged;"[2] and they could say this without apparent absurdity, because it was customary to pardon a culprit if the rope broke after he had been tied up to the gallows, and therefore it was not an uncommon thing to meet with living men who had known what it was to dance upon nothing. The memory of this usage is preserved in a proverbial expression — "The hope of the man that is hanging, that the rope may break"[3] — to signify an exceedingly faint hope. But so much was this indulgence abused that it was abolished by all the parliaments, that of Bordeaux setting the example in 1524, by an edict directing that the sentence should always be, "Hanged until death ensue."

If the cap fits you, wear it.

"Let him that feels itchy, scratch" (French).[4] "Let him wipe his nose that feels the need of it" (French).[5]

Nothing was ever ill said that was not ill taken.

"He who takes [offence] makes [the offence]"

---

[1] Non recordar il capestro in casa dell' impiccato.
[2] Il ne faut pas parler de corde devant un pendu.
[3] L'espoir du pendu, que la corde casse.
[4] Qui se sent galeux, se gratte.
[5] Qui se sent morveux, se mouche.

(Latin).[1] "What do you say 'Hem!' for when I pass?" cries an angry Briton to a Frenchman. "Monsieur Godden," replies the latter, "what for pass you when me say 'Hem?'"

Ye 're busy to clear yourself when naebody files you. — *Scotch.*

That is, you defend yourself when nobody accuses you ; and that looks very suspicious. "He that excuses himself accuses himself" (French).[2]

---

[1] Qui capit, ille facit.
[2] Qui s'excuse, s'accuse.

FALSE APPEARANCES AND PRETENCES, HYPOCRISY, DOUBLE DEALING, TIME-SERVING.

Appearances are deceitful.[1]

"Always judge your fellow passengers to be the opposite of what they strive to appear to be. For instance, a military man is not quarrelsome, for no man doubts his courage; but a snob is. A clergyman is not over strait-laced, for his piety is not questioned; but a cheat is. A lawyer is not apt to be argumentative; but an actor is. A woman that is all smiles and graces is a vixen at heart: snakes fascinate. A stranger that is obsequious and over-civil without apparent cause is treacherous: cats that purr are apt to bite and scratch. Pride is one thing, assumption is another; the latter must always get the cold shoulder, for whoever shews it is no gentleman: men never affect to be what they are, but what they are not. The only man who really is what he appears to be is — a gentleman."[2]

The Livonians say, "The bald pate talks most of hair;" and, "You may freely give a rope to one who talks about hanging."

---

[1] Fronti nulla fides. Schein betrugt.

[2] "Maxims of an Old Stager," by Judge Halliburton.

All is not gold that glitters.

Yellow iron pyrite is as bright as gold, and has often been mistaken for it. The worthless spangles have even been imported at a great cost from California. " Every glowworm is not a fire " (Italian).[1] " Where you think there are flitches of bacon there are not even hooks to hang them on " (Spanish).[2] Many a reputed rich man is insolvent.

Much ado about nothing.

"Great cry and little wool," as the fellow said when he sheared the pig.

"Meikle cry and little woo'," as the deil said when he clipped the sow.—*Scotch.*

" The mountain is in labor, and will bring forth a mouse " (Latin).[3]

Likely lies in the mire, and unlikely gets over.—*Scotch.*

Some from whom great things are expected fail miserably, while others of no apparent mark or promise surprise the world by their success.

You must not hang a man by his looks.

He may be one who is

Like a singed cat, better than likely.

" Under a shabby cloak there is a good tippler " (Spanish).[4]

---

[1] Ogni lucciola non è fuoco.

[2] Adó pensas que hay tocsinos, no hay estacas.

[3] Parturiunt montes, nascetur ridiculus mus.

[4] Debajo de una mala capa hay un buen bebedor.

"Care not" would have it.

Affected indifference is often a trick to obtain an object of secret desire. " I don't want it, I don't want it," says the Spanish friar; " but drop it into my hood." [1] " 'It is nought, it is nought,' saith the buyer; but when he is gone he vaunteth." The girls of Italy, who know how often this artifice is employed in affairs of love, have a ready retort against sarcastic young gentlemen in the adage, " He who finds fault would fain buy." [2]

He that lacks [disparages] my mare would buy my mare. — *Scotch.*

"Sour grapes," said the fox when he could not reach them.

Empty vessels give the greatest sound.

Shaal [shallow] waters mak the maist din. — *Scotch.*

Smooth waters run deep; *or,*

Still waters are deep.

This last proverb, we are told by Quintus Curtius, was current among the Bactrians.[3] The Servians say, " A smooth river washes away its banks ;" the French, " There is no worse water than that which sleeps." [4] " The most covered fire is the strongest " (French) ;" [5] and " Under white ashes there is glowing coal" (Italian).[6]

---

[1] No lo quiero, no lo quiero, mas echad lo en mi capilla.

[2] Chi biasima vuol comprare.

[3] Altissima flumina minimo sono labuntur.

[4] Il n'y a pire eau que l'eau qui dort.

[5] Le feu le plus couvert est le plus ardent.

[6] Sotto la bianca cenere sta la brace ardente.

Where God has his church the devil will have his chapel.

So closely does the shadow of godliness — hypocrisy — wait upon the substance. " Very seldom does any good thing arise but there comes an ugly phantom of a caricature of it, which sidles up against the reality, mouths its favorite words as a third-rate actor does a great part, under-mimics its wisdom, over-acts its folly, is by half the world taken for it, goes some way to suppress it in its own time, and perhaps lives for it in history." [1] Defoe says : —

> " Wherever God erects a house of prayer,
> The devil always builds a chapel there ;
> And 'twill be found upon examination
> The latter has the largest congregation."

The proverb is found in nearly the same form in Italian.[2] The French say, " The devil chants high mass," [3] which reminds us of another English adage, applied by Antonio to Shylock : —

The devil can quote Scripture for his purpose.

" The devil lurks behind the cross," [4] say the Spaniards ; and, " By the vicar's skirts the devil gets up into the belfry." [5]   " O, the slyness of sin," exclaim the

---

[1] " Friends in Council."
[2] Non si tosto si fa un tempio a Dio, che il diavolo ci fabbrica una cappella appresso.
[3] Le diable chante la grande messe.
[4] Detras de la cruz esta el diablo.
[5] Por las haldas del vicario sube el diablo al campanario.

Germans, "that puts an angel before every devil!"[1]
The same thought is expressed by the Queen of Navarre
in her thirteenth novel, where she speaks of "covering
one's devil with the fairest angel."[2]

When the fox preaches beware of the geese.

"The fox preaches to the hens" (French).[3] "When
the devil says his paternosters he wants to cheat you"
(French).[4] "Never spread your wheat in the sun
before the canter's door" (Spanish).[5]

A honey tongue, a heart of gall.

Mouth of ivy, heart of holly. — *Irish.*

He can say, "My jo," an' think it na. — *Scotch.*

Too much courtesy, too much craft.

"The words of a saint, and the claws of a cat"
(Spanish).[6] "The cat is friendly, but scratches"
(Spanish).[7] "Many kiss the hands they would fain see
chopped off" (Arab and Spanish).[8]

He looks as if butter would not melt in his mouth.

Said of a very demure person, sometimes with this
addition, "And yet cheese would not choke him." Of

---

[1] O über die schlaue Sunde, die einen Engel vor jeden Teufel
stellt !

[2] Couvrir son diable du plus bel ange.

[3] Le renard prêche aux poules.

[4] Quand le diable dit ses patenôtres, iu velt te tromper.

[5] Ante la puerta del rezador nunca eches tu trigo al sol.

[6] Palabras de santo, y uñas de gato.

[7] Buen amigo es el gato, sino que rascuña.

[8] Muchos besan manos que quierian ver cortadas.

such a person the Spaniards say, " He looks as if he would not muddy the water."[1] " Nothing is more like an honest man than a rogue " (French).[2]

They 're no a' saints that get holy water. — *Scotch*

" All are not saints who go to church " (Italian).[3]
" Not all who go to church say their prayers " (Italian).[4]
" All are not hunters who blow the horn " (French).[5]
" All are not soldiers who go to the wars " (Spanish).[6]
" All are not princes who ride with the emperor " (Dutch).[7]

The chamber of sickness is the chapel of devotion.

**The devil was sick, the devil a monk would be ;
The devil grew well, the devil a monk was he!**[8]

" All criminals turn preachers when they are under the gallows " (Italian).[9] " The galley is in a bad way when the corsair promises masses and candles " (Spanish).[10]

Satan rebukes sin.[11]

---

[1] Parece que no enturbia el agua.
[2] Rien ne ressemble plus à un honnête homme qu'un fripon.
[3] Non son tutti santi quelli che vanno in chiesa.
[4] Non tutti chi vanno in chiesa fanno orazione.
[5] Ne sont pas tous chasseurs qui sonnent du cor.
[6] Non son soldados todos los que van á la guerra.
[7] Zig zijn niet allen gelijk die met den keizer rijden.
[8] Ægrotat dæmon, monachus tunc esse volebat ;
Dæmon convaluit, dæmon ut ante fuit.
[9] Tutti i rei divengono predicatori quando stanno sotto la forca.
[10] Quando el corsario promete misas y cera, con mal anda ¹ galera.
[11] Claudius accusat mœchos.

The friar preached against stealing when he had a pudding in his sleeve.

According to the Italian account of the affair the friar had a goose in his scapulary on that occasion.[1] " Do as the friar says, and not as he does " (Spanish).[2]

To carry two faces under one hood.

To be what the Romans called " double-tongued," [3] or, in French phrase, " To wear a coat of two parishes." [4] Formerly the parishes in France were bound to supply the army with a certain number of pioneers fully equipped. Every parish claimed the right of clothing its man in its own livery, whence it followed that when two parishes jointly furnished only one man, he was dressed in parti-colored garments, each parish being represented by a moiety which differed from the other in texture and color.

To hold with the hare, and hunt with the hounds.

To be " Jack o' both sides," true to neither. The Romans called this " Sitting on two stools." [5] Liberius Mimus was one of a new batch of senators created by Cæsar. The first day he entered the august assembly, as he was looking about him for a seat, Cicero said to him " I would make room for you were we not so crowded

---

[1] Il frate predicava che non si dovesse robbare, e egli aveva l'occa nel scapulario.

[2] Haz lo que dice el frayle, y no lo que hace.

[3] Homo bilinguis.

[4] Porter un habit de deux paroisses.

[5] Duabus sellis sedere.

together." This was a sly hit at Cæsar, who had packed
the senate with his creatures. Liberius replied, " Ay,
you always liked to sit on two stools."

The Arabs say of a double dealer, " He says to the
thief, ' Steal ; ' and to the house-owner, ' Take care of
thy goods.' " " He howls with the wolves when he is
in the wood, and bleats with the sheep in the field
(Dutch).

If the devil is vicar, you 'll be clerk.
If the deil be laird, you 'll be tenant. — *Scotch.*
The deil ne'er sent a wind out of hell but he wad sail with it. — *Scotch.*
The vicar of Bray will be vicar of Bray still.

Simon Aleyn, or Allen, held the vicarage of Bray, in
Berkshire, for fifty years, in the reigns of Henry VIII.,
Edward VI., Mary, and Elizabeth, and was always of
the religion of the sovereign for the time being. First
he was a Papist, then a Protestant, afterwards a Papist,
and a Protestant again ; yet he would by no means
admit that he was a turncoat. " No," said he, " I have
always stuck to my principle, which is this — to live and
die vicar of Bray." His consistency has been celebrated
in a song, the burden of which is —

> " For this is law I will maintain —
> Unto my dying day, sir,
> Whatever king in England reign,
> I'll be the vicar of Bray, sir."

---

[1] Hij huilt met de wolven waarmede hij en het bosch is, en
blaat met de schapen in het veld.

" Such are men, now o' days," says Fuller, " who, though they cannot turn the wind, they turn their mills, and set them so that wheresoever it bloweth, their grist should certainly be grinded."

During the Peninsular war many signboards over shops and hotels in Spanish towns had on one side the arms of France, and on the other those of Spain, which were turned as best suited the interests of their owners and the feelings of the troops which alternately occupied the place.

It is hard to sit at Rome and fecht wi' the pope. — *Scotch.*

Prudence forbids us to engage in strife with those in whose power we are. Oriental servility goes further than this. Bernier tells us that it was a current proverb in the dominions of the Great Mogul, " If the king saith at noonday, 'It is night,' you are to say, 'Behold the moon and stars!'" The Egyptians say, " When the monkey reigns dance before him." The philosopher desisted from controversy with the Emperor Hadrian, confessing himself unable to cope in argument with the master of thirty legions.

There 's nae gude in speaking ill o' the laird within his ain bounds. — *Scotch.*

On this principle Baillie Nicol Jarvie thinks it well, when passing the Fairies' Hill, to call them, as others do, men of peace, meaning thereby to conciliate their good-will. " Speak not ill of a great enemy," says Selden, " but rather give him good words, that he may

use you the better if you chance to fall into his hands.
The Spaniard did this when he was dying. His confessor told him (to work him to repentance) how the
devil tormented the wicked that went to hell. The
Spaniard replying, called the devil ' my lord.' ' I hope
my lord the devil is not so cruel.' His confessor re-
proved him. ' Excuse me,' said the don, ' for calling
him so. I know not into what hands I may fall; and
if I happen into his, I hope he will use me the better
for giving him good words.' "

It is good to have friends everywhere.
It 's gude to hae friends baith in heaven and hell. — *Scotch.*

Brantôme relates that Robert de la Mark had a
painting executed in which were represented St. Margaret and the devil, with himself on his knees before
them, a candle in each hand, and a scroll issuing from
his mouth, containing these words : " If God will not
aid me, the devil surely will not fail me." This is quite
in the spirit of Virgil's line, " If I cannot bend the
celestials to my purpose, I will move hell."[1] Others
besides De la Mark have thought it prudent " To offer a
candle to God and another to the devil" (French) ;[2]
or, " A candle to St. Michael and one to his devil "
(French),[3] lest the time might come when the devil
under the archangel's feet should get the upper hand.

---

[1] Flectere si nequeo superos, Acheronta movebo.
[2] Donner une chandelle à Dieu, et une au diable.
[3] Donner une chandelle à Saint Michel, et une à son diable.

Upon the same principle a discreet person in the early Christian times took care never to pass a prostrate statue of Jupiter without saluting it.

One must sometimes hold a candle to the devil.

OPPORTUNITY.

What may be done at any time, will be done at no time.

" By the street of By-and-by, one arrives at the house of Never " (Spanish).[1]

Never put off till to-morrow what you can do to-day.

" One to-day is worth ten to-morrows " (German).[2] " To-day must borrow nothing of to-morrow" (German).[3] " When God says to-day, the devil says to-morrow" (German).[4] Talleyrand used to reverse these maxims : by never doing to-day what he could put off till to-morrow, he avoided committing himself prematurely.

Strike while the iron is hot.

This proverb is cosmopolitan : but

Make hay while the sun shines,

is peculiar to England, and, as Trench remarks, could have had its birth only under such variable skies as ours.

---

[1] Por la calle de despues se va á la casa de nunca.
[2] Ein Heute ist besser als zehn Morgen.
[3] Heute muss dem Morgen nichts borgen.
[4] Wenn Gott sagt : Heute, sagt der Teufel : Morgen.

Take the ball at the hop.

Take time while time is, for time will away.

Time and tide wait for no man.

"God keep you from 'It is too late'" (Spanish).[1] "A little too late, much too late" (Dutch).[2] "Stay but a while, you lose a mile" (Dutch).[3]

After a delay comes a let.

Delays are dangerous.

Especially in affairs of love and marriage. Therefore, "When thy daughter's chance comes, wait not her father's coming from the market" (Spanish).[4] Close with the offer on the spot. "When the fool has made up his mind, the market has gone by" (Spanish).[5]

He that will not when he may,

When he will he shall have nay.

"Some refuse roast meat, and afterwards long for the smoke of it" (Italian).[6]

The nearer the church, the farther from God.

"Next to the minister, last to mass" (French).[7] "The

---

[1] Guarde te Dios de hecho es

[2] Een wenig te laat, veel te laat.

[3] Sta maar een wijl, gij verliest een mijl.

[4] Quando a tu hija le veniere su hado, no aguardes que vienga su padre del mercado.

[5] Quando el necio es acordado, el mercado es ya pasado.

[6] Tal lascia l'arrostó, chi poi ne brama il fumo. Qui refuse, muse.

[7] Près du monstier, à messe le dernier.

nearer to Rome, the worse Christian " (Dutch).[1] The buyer of many books will probably read few of them ; and somebody has said that he never was afraid of engaging in a controversy with the owner of a large library. Many a Londoner would never see half its lions but for the necessity of showing them to country cousins.

The shoemaker's wife goes worst shod.

Where the best wine is made, the worst is commonly drunk. Better fish is to be had in Billingsgate than on the seacoast.

---

[1] Hoe digter bij Rom, hoe slechter Christ.

UNCERTAINTY OF THE FUTURE.—HOPE.

Man proposes, God disposes.[1]

"There's a divinity that shapes men's ends,
Rough hew them how they will."

He that reckons without his host must reckon again.

Don't reckon your chickens before they are hatched.

Some of the eggs may be addled. Remember the story of Alnaschar.

Sune enough to cry " chick " when it's out o' the shell.— *Scotch.*

Gut nae fish till ye get them.— *Scotch.*

" Cry no herring till you have it in the net " (Dutch).[2]
" First catch your hare," says Mrs. Glasse, and then you
may settle how you will have it cooked. The Greeks
and Romans thought it not wise " To sing triumph before the victory." [3] It is a rash bargain " To sell the
bird on the bough " (Italian) ; [4] or, " The bearskin be-

---

[1] In French, L'homme propose, Dieu dispose ; in German, Man
denkt's, Gott lenkt's. The Spanish form is a little different : Los
dichos en nos, los hechos en Dios.

[2] Roep geen haring eer hij in 't net is.

[3] Ante victoriam canere triumphum.

[4] Vender l'uccello in su la frasca.

fore you have caught the bear " (Italian),[1] as Æsop has demonstrated. Finally, " Unlaid eggs are uncertain chickens " (German) [2]

> Praise a fair day at night.
>
> It is not good praising a ford till a man be over.
>
> Don't halloo till you are out of the wood.

" Don't cry ' Hey! ' till you are over the ditch " (German).[3] " Look to the end " (Latin).[4] " No man can with certainty be called happy before his death," as the Grecian sage told Crœsus. " Call me not olive till you see me gathered " (Spanish).[5]

> To build castles in the air.

To let imagination beguile us with visionary prospects. The metaphor is intelligible to everybody, but that in the French equivalent, " To build castles in Spain." [6] requires explanation. The Abbè Morrellet ascribes the origin of this phrase to the general belief in the boundless wealth of Spain after she had become mistress of the mines of Mexico and Peru. This is plausible, but wrong; for the " Roman de la Rose," which was published long before the discovery of America, contains this line, *Lors feras chasteaulx en Espagne.* M. Quitard

---

[1] Non vender la pelle dell' orso prima di pigliarlo.

[2] Ungelegte Eier sind ungewisse Hünnlein.

[3] Rufe nicht " Juch ! " bis du über den Graben bist.

[4] Respice finem.

[5] No me dignas oliva hasta que me veas cogida.

[6] Faire des châteaux en Espagne.

says that the proverb dates from the latter part of the eleventh century, when Henri de Bourgogne crossed the Pyrenees, at the head of a great number of knights, to win glory and plunder from the Infidels, and received from Alfonso, king of Castile, in reward for his services, the hand of that sovereign's daughter, Theresa, and the county of Lusitania, which, under his son Alfonso Henriquez, became the kingdom of Portugal. The success of these illustrious adventurers excited the emulation of the warlike French nobles, and set every man dreaming of fiefs to be won, and castles to be built, in Spain. Similar feelings had been awakened some years before by the conquest of England by William of Normandy, and then the French talked proverbially of " Building castles in Albany," [1] that is, in Albion. It is worthy of remark that previously to the eleventh century there were hardly any castles built in Christian Spain, or by the Saxons in England. The new adventurers had to build for themselves.

Don't tell the devil too much of your mind.

Be not too forward to proclaim your intentions. "Tell your business, and leave the devil alone to do it for you" (Italian).[2] " A wise man," Selden tells us, " should never resolve upon anything — at least, never let the world know his resolution; for if he cannot arrive at that, he is ashamed. How many things did

---

[1] Faire des chasteaulx en Albanie.
[2] Dì il fatto tuo, e lascia far al diavolo.

the king resolve, in his declaration concerning Scotland, never to do, and yet did them all! A man must do according to accidents and emergencies. Never tell your resolutions beforehand, but when the cast is thrown play it as well as you can to win the game you are at. 'Tis but folly to study how to play size ace when you know not whether you shall throw it or no." "Muddy though it be, say not, 'Of this water I will not drink,'" (Spanish).[1] "There is no use in saying, 'Such a way I will not go, or such water I will not drink'" (Italian).[2]

There's many a slip 'twixt the cup and the lip.

"Between the hand and the mouth the soup is often spilt" (French).[3] "Wine poured out is not swallowed" (French).[4] These three proverbs are derived from the same Greek original, the English one being nearest to it in form. A king of Samos tasked his slaves unmercifully in laying out a vineyard, and one of them, exasperated by this ill usage, prophesied that his master would never drink of the wine of that vineyard. Eager to confute this prediction, the king took the first grapes produced by his vines, pressed them into a cup in the slave's presence, and derided him as a false prophet. The slave replied, "Many things happen

---

1 Por tubia que esté, no digas desta agua no bebere.
2 Non giova a dire per tal via non passero, ni di tal acqua bevero.
3 De la main a la bouche se perd souvent la soupe.
4 Vin versé n'est pass avalé.

between the cup and the lip;" and these words became
a proverb, for just then a cry was raised that a wild
boar had broken into the vineyard, and the king, setting
down the untasted cup, went to meet the beast, and was
killed in the encounter.

> God send you readier meat than running hares.
> A bird in the hand is worth two in the bush.
> Better a wren in the hand than a crane in the air.
> — *Irish and French.*[1]

Cranes were in much request for the table down to
the end of the fourteenth century, if not later. " Better
a leveret in the kitchen than a wild boar in the forest "
(Livonian). " Better is an egg to-day than a pullet to-
morrow " (Italian).[2] " One here-it-is is better than two
you-shall-have-it's " (French).[3]

> Possession is nine points of the law.

And there are only ten of them in all. Others
reckon possession as eleven points, the whole number
being twelve. " Him that is in possession God helps "
(Italian).[4] " Possession is as good as title " (French).[5]

> I'll not change a cottage in possession for a kingdom in reversion.
> Better haud by a hair nor draw by a tether. — *Scotch.*

---

[1] Moineau en main vaut mieux que grue qui vole.
[2] E meglio aver oggi un uovo che domani una gallina.
[3] Mieux vaut un tenez que deux vous l'aurez.
[4] A chi è in tenuta, Dio gli aiuta.
[5] Possession vaut titre.

He that waits for dead men's shoes may long go barefoot.

He gaes lang barefoot that wears dead men's shoon.—*Scotch.*

" He hauls at a long rope who desires another's death " (French).[1] " He who waits for another's trencher eats a cold meal "(Catalan).[2]

Live, horse, and you'll get grass.[3]

" Die not, O mine ass, for the Spring is coming, and with it clover " (Turkish). Unfortunately, " For the hungry, *wait* is a hard word " (German) ; [4] and

While the grass grows the steed starves.

The old horse may die waiting for new grass.

Hope holds up the head.

Hope is the bread of the unhappy.

Were it not for hope the heart would break.

He that lives on hope has a slim diet.

Aubrey relates that Lord Bacon, being in York House garden, looking on fishers as they were throwing their net, asked them what they would take for their draught. They answered so much. His lordship would offer them only so much. They drew up their net, and in it were only two or three little fishes. His lordship then told them it had been better for them to have taken his offer. They replied, they hoped to have had a better draught ; but, said his lordship, —

---

[1] A longue corde tire, qui d'autrui mort désire.
[2] Qui escudella d'altri espera, freda la menja.
[3] In Italian, Caval non morire, che erba da venire.
[4] Dem Hungrigen ist " Harr " ein hart Wort.

"Hope is a good breakfast, but a bad supper."

"Hope and expectation are a fool's income" (Danish).[1]

Hopes deferred hang the heart on tenter-hooks.

"He gives twice who gives quickly" (Latin) ;[2] and "A prompt refusal has in part the grace of a favor granted" (Latin).[3]

All is not at hand that helps.

We cannot foresee whence-help may come to us, nor always trace back to their sources the advantages we actually enjoy. "Water comes to the mill from afar" (Portugese).[4] On the other hand, "Far water does not put out near fire" (Italian) ;[5] and "Better is a near neighbor than a distant cousin" (Italian).[6] "Friends living far away are no friends" (Greek).[7]

---

[1] Haabe og vente er Giekerente

[2] Bis dat, qui cito dat.

[3] Pars est beneficii quod petitur si cito neges. — *Publius Syrus.*

[4] De lomge vem agoa a o momho.

[5] Acqua lontana non spegne il fuoco vicino.

[6] Meglio un prossimo vicino che un lontano cugino.

[7] Τηλου ναιοντες φιλοι ουκ εισι φιλοι.

EXPERIENCE.

Bought wit is best.

Wit once bought is worth twice taught.

Hang a dog on a crabtree, and he'll never love verjuice.

A burnt child dreads the fire.

Fear is so imaginative that it starts even at the ghost of a remembered danger. "A scalded dog dreads cold water" (French, Italian, Spanish).[1] "A dog which has been beaten with a stick is afraid of its shadow" (Italian).[2] "Whom a serpent has bitten, a lizard alarms" (Italian).[3] "One who has been bitten by a serpent is afraid of a rope" (Hebrew). "The man who has been beaten with a firebrand runs away at the sight of a firefly" (Cingalese). "He that has been wrecked shudders even at still water" (Ovid).[4]

Experience is the mistress of fools.

She keeps a dear school, says Poor Richard ; but fools will learn in no other, and scarce in that. "An

---

[1] Chat échaudé craint l'eau froide.
[2] Il can battuto dal bastone, ha paura dell' ombra.
[3] Chi della serpa è punto, ha paura della lucertola.
[4] Tranquillas etiam naufragus horret aquas.

ass does not stumble twice over the same stone"
(French).[1] "Unfairly does he blame Neptune who
suffers shipwreck a second time" (Publius Syrus).[2]

He that will not be ruled by the rudder must be ruled by the rock.
—*Cornish.*

Better learn frae your neebor's scathe than frae your ain. —*Scotch.*

Wise men learn by others' harms, fools by their own,
like Epimetheus, the Greek personification of afterwit.[3]
"Happy he who is made wary by others' perils"
(Latin).[4]

Old birds are not to be caught with chaff.

"Old crows are hard to catch" (German).[5] "New
nets don't catch old birds" (Italian).[6]

I'm ower auld a cat to draw a strae [straw] afore my nose.—*Scotch.*

That is, I am not to be gulled. A kitten will jump
at a straw drawn before her, but a cat that knows the
world is not to be fooled in that way.

Don't tell new lies to old rouges.

He that cheats me ance, shame fa' him; if he cheats me twice,
shame fa' me. — *Scotch.*

It is a silly fish that is caught twice with the same bait.

The French have a humerous equivalent for this

---

[1] Un âne ne trébuche pas deux fois sur la même pierre.
[2] Improbe Neptunum accusat qui iterum naufragium facit.
[3] Ὃς ἐπεί κακὸν ἔχε νόησε.
[4] Felix quem faciunt aliena pericula cautum.
[5] Alte Krähen sind schwer zu fangen.
[6] Nuova rete non piglia uccello vecchio.

proverb, growing out of the following story: A young
rustic told his priest at confession that he had broken
down a neighbor's hedge to get at a blackbird's nest.
The priest asked if he had taken away the young birds.
" No," said he ; " they were hardly grown enough. I
will let them alone until Saturday evening." No more
was said on the subject, but when Saturday evening
came, the young fellow found the nest empty, and
readily guessed who it was that had forestalled him.
The next time he went to confession he had to tell
something in which a young girl was partly concerned.
" Oh ! " said his ghostly father ; " how old is she ? "
" Seventeen." " Good-looking ? "   "The prettiest girl
in the village."   " What is her name?   Where does
she live ? " the confessor hastily inquired ; and then
he got for an answer the phrase which has passed into a
proverb, " A d'autres, dénicheur de merles ! " which
may be paraphrased, " Try that upon somebody else,
Mr. filcher of blackbirds,"

When an old dog barks, look out.

" An old dog does not bark for nothing " (Italian).[1]
" There is no hunting but with old hounds " (French).[2]

Live and learn.

The langer we live the mair ferlies [wonders] we see. — *Scotch.*

Adversity makes a man wise, not rich.

---

[1] Cane vecchio non baia indarno.
[2] Il n'est chasse que de vieux chiens.

" Wind in the face makes a man wise " (French).[1]

A smooth sea never made a skilful mariner.

It is hard to halt before a cripple.

It is hard to counterfeit lameness successfully in presence of a real cripple. " He who is of the craft can discourse about it " (Italian).[2] " Don't talk Latin before clerks " (French),[3] or " Arabic in the Moor's house " (Spanish).[4]

The proof of the pudding is in the eating.

" Do not judge of the ship while it is on the stocks " (Italian).

War's sweet to them that never tried it.

---

[1] Vent au visage rend un homme sage.
[2] Chi è dell'arte, prò ragionar della.
[3] Il ne faut pas parler latin devant les clercs.
[4] In casa del moro no hablar algarabia.
[5] Non giudicar la nave stando in terra.

CHOICE. DILEMMA. COMPARISON.

Pick and choose, and take the worst.

The lass that has mony wooers aft wales [chooses] the warst.

—*Scotch.*

Refuse a wife with one fault, and take one with two. — *Welsh.*

" He that has a choice has trouble " (Dutch).[1] " He that chooses takes the worst " (French).[2]

Of two evils choose the least.

Where bad is the best, naught must be the choice.

A traveller in America, inquiring his way, was told there were two roads, one long, and the other short, and that it mattered not which he took. Surprised at such a direction, he asked, " Can there be a doubt about the choice between the long and the short?" and the answer was, " Why, no matter which of the two you take, you will not have gone far in it before you will wish from the bottom of your heart that you had taken t'other."

"There's ne'er a best among them," as the fellow said of the fox cubs.

---

[1] Die keur heeft, heeft angst.

[2] Qui choisit prend le pire.

As good eat the devil as the broth he's boiled in.

Cut of the fryingpan into the fire.

To escape from one evil and incur another as bad or worse is an idea expressed in many proverbial metaphors; *e. g.*, "To come out of the rain under the spout" (German).[1] "Flying from the bull, I fell into the river" (Spanish).[2] "To break the constable's head and take refuge with the sheriff" (Spanish).[3] "To shun Charybdis and strike upon Scylla" is a well-known phrase, which almost everybody supposes to have been current among the ancients. It is not to be found, however, in any classical author, but appears for the first time in the Alexandriad of Philip Gaultier, a medieval Latin poet. In his fifth book he thus apostrophizes Darius when flying from Alexander: —

> "Nescis, heu! perdite, nescis
> Quem fugias : hostes incurris dum fugis hostem ;
> Incidis in Scyllam cupiens vitare Charybdim."

Go forward, and fall; go backward, and mar all.

"A precipice ahead, wolves behind" (Latin).[4] "To be between the hammer and the anvil" (French).[5]

You may go farther and fare worse.

To be between the devil and the deep sea.

---

1 Aus dem hegen unter die Traufe kommen.
2 Huyendo del toro, cayó en el arroyo.
3 Descalabrar el alguacil, y accogerse al corregidor.
4 A fronte præcipitium, a tergo lupi.
5 Etre entre le marteau et l'enclume

The one-eyed is a king in the land of the blind.

" A substitute shines brightly as a king
Until a king be by."

" Where there are no dogs the fox is a king " (Italian).[1]

They that be in hell think there is no other heaven.
It is good to have two strings to one's bow.
It is good riding at two anchors.
He is no fox that hath but one hole.
The mouse that has but one hole is soon caught.[2]
Do not put all your eggs in one basket;

nor "too many of them under one hen" (Dutch).[3]
" Hang not all upon one nail " (German),[4] nor risk
your whole fortune upon one venture.

Comparisons are odious.

---

[1] Dove non sono i cani, la volpe è re.
[2] Mus uni non fidit antro.—*Plautus.*
[3] Man moet niet te viel eijeren onder eene hen leggen.
[4] Henke nicht alles auf einen Nagel.

SHIFTS.—CONTRIVANCES.—STRAINED USES.

A bad shift is better than none.

Better sup wi' a cutty nor want a spune.—*Scotch.*

A cutty is a spoon with a stumpy handle or none at all. It is not a very convenient implement, but it will serve at a pinch.

A bad bush is better than the open field.

A wee bush is better nor nae bield.—*Scotch.*

Bield, shelter. A man's present occupation may not be lucrative, or his connections as serviceable as he could wish, but he should not therefore quit them until he has better.

Half a loaf is better than no bread.

I will make a shaft or a bolt of it.

A shaft is an arrow for the longbow, a bolt is for the crossbow.

If I canna do it by might I'll do it by slight.—*Scotch.*

" It's best no to be rash," said Edie Ochiltree —

Sticking disna gang by strengh, but by the guiding o' the gully.
—*Scotch.*

A gully is a butcher's knife. There is a knack even in slaughtering a pig.

There goes reason to the roasting of eggs.

Many ways to kill a dog besides hanging him.

A story told by the African traveller, Richardson, supplies an apt illustration of this proverb. An Arab woman preferred another man to her husband, and frankly confessed that her affections had strayed. Her lord, instead of flying into a passion and killing her on the spot, thought a moment, and said, "I will consent to divorce you if you will promise me one thing." "What is that?" the wife eagerly asked. "You must *looloo* to me only on your wedding day." This *looloo* is a peculiar cry with which it is customary for brides to salute any handsome passer-by. The woman gave the promise required, the divorce took place, and the marriage followed. On the day of the ceremony the ex-husband passed the camel on which the bride rode, and gave her the usual salute by discharging his firelock, in return for which she loolooed to him according to promise. The new bridegroom, enraged at this marked preference — for he noticed that she had not greeted any one else — and suspecting that he was duped, instantly fell upon the bride and slew her. He had no sooner done so than her brothers came up and shot him dead, so that the first husband found himself amply avenged without having endangered himself in the slightest degree. "Contrivance is

better than force" (French).[1] Lysander of Sparta was
reproached for relying too little on open valor in war,
and too much on ruses not always worthy of a de-
scendant of Hercules. He replied, in allusion to the
skin of the Nemæan beast worn by his great ancestor,
"Where the lion's skin comes short we must eke it out
with the fox's."

> It is easy to find a stick to beat a dog ; *or,*
> It is easy to find a stone to throw at a dog.

It is easy for the strong to find an excuse for maltreating the weak. "On a little pretext the wolf
seizes the sheep" (French),[2] or the lamb, as the fable
shows. "If you want to flog your dog say he ate the
poker" (Spanish).[3] "If a man wants to thrash his
wife, let him ask her for drink in the sunshine"
(Spanish),[4] for then what can be easier for him than
to pick a quarrel with her about the motes in the
clearest water?

> A handsaw is a good thing, but not to shave with.

Everything to its proper use. In Italy they say, "With
the gospel sometimes one becomes a heretic." Disraeli,
and after him Dean Trench, have given to this proverb
an erroneous interpretation, founded on a false reading.
Their version of it is " Coll ' Evangelo si diventa heret-

---

[1] Mieux vaut engin que force.
[2] A petite achoison le loup prend le mouton.
[3] Para axotar el perro, que se come el hierro.
[4] Quien quiere dar palos á su muger, pidele al sol á bever.

ico." Here there is no qualifying "sometimes;" the proposition is put absolutely, and the two English writers consider it to be a popular confession that the maintenence of the Romish system and the study of Holy Scripture cannot go together." It would certainly be " not a little remarkable," if it were true, " that such a confession should have embodied itself in the popular utterances of the nation ; " but the fact is that nothing more is meant by the proverb than what the Inquisition itself might sanction, It is only a pointed way of saying that anything, however good, is liable to be used mischievously.[1]

---

[1] " Con l' Evangelo talvolta si diventa eretico" is the original, as given by Toriano in his folio collection of Italian proverbs, London, 1666. In Giusti's " Raccolta," etc., Firenza, 1853, we read, " Col Vangelo si può diventar eretici," to which the editor appeands this gloss, " Ogni cosa può torcersi male."

ADVICE.

He that will not be counselled cannot be helped.

"He who will not go to heaven needs preaching"
(German).[1] "He that will not hear must feel" (German).[2]

Two heads are better than one.

"Four eyes see more than two" (Spanish) ;[3] and
"More know the pope and a peasant than than the pope
alone," [4] as they say in Venice.

Come na to the counsel unca'd.—*Scotch.*

"Never give advice unasked " (German).[5]

Every one thinks himself able to advise another.

"Nothing is given so freely as advice" (French).[6]
" Of judgment every one has a stock for sale" (Italian).[7]

---

[1] Wer nicht in den Himmel will, braucht keine Predigt.
[2] Wer nicht hören will, muss fühlen.
[3] Mas veen quatro ojos que dos.
[4] Sa più il papa e un contadino che il papa solo.
[5] Rathe Niemand ungebeten.
[6] Rien ne se donne aussi libéralement que les conseils.
[7] Del judizio ognun ne vende.

He that kisseth his wife in the market-place shall have people enough to teach him.

" He who builds according to every man's advice will have a crooked house " (Danish).[1]

He that speers a' opinions comes ill speed.—*Scotch.*

" If you want to get into the bog ask five fools the way to the wood " (Livonian). " Take help of many, counsel of few " (Danish).[2]

A fool may put something in a wise man's head.

It was a saying of Cato the elder, that wise men learnt more by fools than fools by wise men.

---

[1] Hvo som bygger efter hver Mands Raad, hans Huser kommer kroget at staae.

[2] Tag Mange til Hielp og Faa til Rad.

DETRACTION. — CALUMNY. — COMMON FAME. — GOOD REPUTE.

The smoke follows the fairest.

The original of this is in Aristophanes : it means that

"Envy doth merit like its shade pursue."

" The best bearing trees are the most beaten " (Italian).[1] " It is only at the tree laden with fruit that people throw stones" (French).[2] " Towers," say the Chinese, " are measured by their shadows, and great men by their calumniators." An old French proverb compares detraction to dogs that bark only at the full moon, and never heed her in the quarter. " If the fool has a hump," say the Livonians, " no one notices it ; if the wise man has a pimple, everybody talks about it."

Slander leaves a slur.

" A blow of a fryingpan smuts, if it does not hurt "

---

[1] I megliori alberi sono i più battuti.

[2] On ne jette des pierres qu'à l'arbre chargé de fruits.

(Spanish).[1] The Arabs say, " Take a bit of mud, dab it against the wall: if it does not stick it will leave its mar'; " and we have a similar proverb derived from the Latin : [2] —

> Throw much dirt, and some will stick.

Fortunately

> When the dirt's dry it will rub out.
> Ill-will never spoke well.

The evidence of a prejudiced witness is to be distrusted. " He that is an enemy to the bride does not speak well of the wedding" (Spanish) ; [3] and " A runaway monk never spoke in praise of his monastery" (Italian).[4]

> Give a dog an ill name and hang him.

> "I'll not beat thee nor abuse thee," said the Quaker to his dog :
> " but I'll give thee an ill name."—*Irish.*

> He that hath an ill name is half-hanged.

A French proverb declares, with a still bolder figure, that " Report hangs the man." [5] The Spaniards say, " Whoso wants to kill his dog has but to charge him with madness." [6]

> All are not thieves that dogs bark at.

The innocent are sometimes cried down.   " An honest

---

[1] El glope de la sarten, aunque no duele, tizna.
[2] Calumniare audacter, aliquid adhærebit.
[3] El que es enemigo de la novia no dice bien de la boda.
[4] Monaco vagabondo non disse mai lode del suo monastero.
[5] Le bruit pend l'homme.
[6] Quien á su perro quiere matas, rabia le ha de levantar.

man is not the worse because a dog barks at him"
(Danish).[1] "What cares lofty Diana for the barking
dog?" (Latin).[2]

> Common fame is seldom to blame.
>
> What everybody says must be true.
>
> It never smokes but there's a fire.

"There's never a cry of 'Wolf' but the wolf is in the
district" (Italian).[3] "There's never much talk of a thing
but there's some truth in it" (Italian).[4] This is the
sense in which our droll English saying is applied : —

> "There was a thing in it!" quoth the fellow when he drank the
> dishclout.

To accept the last half-dozen of proverbs too absolutely
would often lead us to uncharitable conclusions; we
must, therefore, temper our belief in these maxims by
means of their opposites, such as this : —

> Common fame is a common liar.

"Heresay is half lies" (German, Italian).[5] "Hear the
other side, and believe little" (Italian).[6]

---

[1] Ærlig Mand er ei disværre, at en Hund göer ad ham.

[2] Latrantem curatne alta Diana canem?

[3] E' non si grida mai al lupo, che non sia in paese.

[4] Non si dice mai tanto una cosa che non sia qualche cosa.

[5] Hörensagen ist halb gelogen. Aver sentito dire è mezza buggia.

[6] Odi l'altra parte, e credi poco.

A tale never loses in the telling.

Witness George Colman's story of the Three Black Crows.

The devil is not so black as he is painted.

Nor is the lion so fierce (Spanish).[1] " Report makes the wolf bigger than he is" (German).[2]

It is a sin to belie the devil.

Give the devil his due.

If one's name be up he may lie in bed.

" Get a good name and go to sleep" (Spanish).[3] So do many. Hence it is often better to intrust the execution of a work to be done to an obscure man than to one whose reputation is established.

One man may better steal a horse than another look over the hedge.

" A good name covers theft" (Spanish).[4] " The honest man enjoys the theft " (Spanish).[5]

A gude name is sooner tint [lost] than won.—*Scotch.*

" Once in folks' mouths, hardly ever well out of them again" (German).[6] " Good repute is like the cypress : once cut, it never puts forth leaf again" (Italian).[7]

---

[1] No es tan bravo el leon como le pintan.
[2] Geschrei macht den Wolf grösser als er ist.
[3] Cobra buena fama, y échate á dormir.
[4] Buena fama hurto encubre.
[5] El buen hombre goza el hurto.
[6] Einmal in der Leute Mund, kommt man übel wieder heraus.
[7] La buona fama è come il cipresso : una volta tagliato non riverdisce più.

TRUTH. — FALSEHOOD. — HONESTY.

A lie has no legs.

A proverb of eastern origin, meaning that a lie has no stability : wrestle with it, and down it goes. The Italians and Spaniards say, "A lie has short legs;"[1] and in the same sense, "A liar is sooner caught than a cripple."[2] He trips up his own heels.

Liars should have good memories.

"Memory in a liar is no more than needs," says Fuller. "For, first, lies are hard to be remembered, because many, whereas truth is but one : secondly, because a lie cursorily told takes little footing and settled fatness in the teller's memory, but prints itself deeper in the hearer's, who takes the greater notice because of the improbability and deformity thereof; and one will remember the sight of a monster longer than the sight of a handsome body. Hence comes it to pass that when the liar hath forgotten himself his auditors put him in mind of the lie, and take him therein."

---

[1] La mentira tiene cortas las piernas. Le bugie hanno corte le gambe.

[2] Si arriva più presto un bugiardo che un zoppo.

11

Fair fall truth and daylight.

Speak truth and shame the devil.

Truth and honesty keep the crown o' the causey. — *Scotch.*

They march boldly along the middle of the roadway which was formerly the place of honor for pedestrians in Scottish towns. " Truth seeks no corners" (Latin).[1]

Truth may be blamed, but shall ne'er be ashamed.

" It is mighty, and will prevail" (Latin).[2] "It is God's daughter" (Spanish).[3] "Truth and oil always come to the surface" (Spanish).[4] " It takes a good many shovel-fuls of earth to bury the truth" (German).[5]

Plain dealing is a jewel, but they that use it die beggars.

" He that speaks the truth must have one foot in the stirrup," say the Turks, who are a people by no means addicted to lying. " People praise truth, but invite lying to be their guest " (Lettish). " My gossips dislike me because I tell them the truth" (Spanish).[6]

Truth has a good face, but ragged clothes.

He that follows truth too near the heels will have dirt kicked in his face.

---

1 Veritas non quærit angulos.

2 Magna est veritas et prævalebit.

3 La verdad es hija de Dios.

4 La verdad, como el olio, siempre anda en somo.

5 Zum Begräbniss der Wahrheit gehören viel Schaufeln.

6 Mal me quieren mis comadres, porque les digo las verdades.

Honesty is the best policy.

Is it Charles Lamb who says that a rogue is a fool with a circumbendibus?

An honest man's word is as good as his bond.

And better than what is called " Connaught security : three in a bond and a book oath."

SPEECH.—SILENCE.

Speech is silvern, silence is golden.

" Be silent, or say something that is better than silence" (German).[1] " Better silence than ill speech" (Swedish).[2] " Talking comes by nature, silence of understanding" (German).[3] " Who speaks, sows ; who keeps silence, reaps" (Italian).[4]

Silence seldom does harm.

Least said, soonest mended.

The principle applies still more forcibly to writing. " Words fly, writing remains" (Latin).[5] A man's spoken words may be unnoticed, or forgotten, or denied ; but what he has put down in black and white is tangible evidence against him. Therefore " Think much, say little, write less" (Italian).[6] Give Cardinal Richelieu two lines

---

[1] Schweig, oder rede etwas das besser ist denn Schweigen.
[2] Bättre tyga än illa tala.
[3] Reden kommt von Natur, Schweigen von Verstunde.
[4] Chi parla, semina ; chi tace, raccoglie.
[5] Verba volant, scripta manent.
[6] Pensa molto, parla poco, scrivi meno.

of any man's writing and he needed no more to hang him. Fabio Merto, an archbishop of the seventeenth century, has oddly remarked, " It is nowhere mentioned in the Gospels that our Lord wrote more than once, and then it was on the sand, in order that the wind might efface the writing." " Silence was never written down" (Italian) ; [1] and " A silent man's words are not brought into court" (Danish).[2] " Hear, see, and say nothing, if you wish to live in peace" (Italian).[3]

A fool's tongue is long enough to cut his own throat.

" Let not the tongue say what the head shall pay for" (Spanish).[4] " The sheep that bleats is strangled by the wolf" (Italian).[5] " He that knows nothing knows enough if he knows how to be silent" (Italian).[6]

A fool's bolt is soon shot.

" A foolish judge passes quick sentence" (French).[7] " He who knows little soon sings it out " (Spanish).[8]

When a fool has spoken he has done all.

" It is always the worst wheel that creaks" (French,

---

[1] Il tacere non fu mai scritto.
[2] Tiende Mands Ord komme ei til Tinge.
[3] Odi, vedi, e taci, se vuoi viver in pace.
[4] No diga la lengua por do paque la cabeza.
[5] Pecora che bella, il lupo la strozza.
[6] Assai sa, chi non sa, se tacer sa.
[7] De fol juge brève sentence.
[8] Quien poco sabe, presto lo reza.

Italian).[1] The shallowest persons are the most loquacious.
" Were fools silent they would pass for wise " (Dutch).[2]

Silence gives consent.

" Silence answers much" (Dutch).[3]

A man may hold his tongue in an ill time.

" Amyclæ was undone by silence " (Latin).[4] The
citizens having been often frightened with false news of the
enemy's coming, made it penal for any one to report such
a thing in future. Hence, when the enemy did come
indeed, they were surprised and taken. There is a time
to speak as well as to be silent.

Spare to speak and spare to speed.

" If the child does not cry the mother does not understand it" (Russian). " Him that speaks not, God hears
not" (Spanish).[5]

---

1 C'est toujours la plus mauvaise roue qui crie. E la peggior
ruota quella che fa più rumore.
2 Zweegen de dwazen zij waren wijs.
3 Zwijgen antwoordt veel.
4 Amyclas silentium perdidit.
5 A quien no habla, no le oye Dios.

THREATENING.—BOASTING.

The greatest barkers bite not sorest.
Great barkers are nae biters. — *Scotch*.

THOSE who threaten most loudly are not the most to be feared. "Timid dogs bark worse than they bite" (Latin),[1] was a proverb of the Bactrians, as Quintus Curtius informs us. The Turks say, "The dog barks, but the caravan passes." "What matters the barking of the dog that does not bite?" (German);[2] but "Beware of a silent dog and of still water" (Latin).[3] "The silent dog bites first" (German).[4] "A fig for our democrats!" Horace Walpole wrote in 1792: "Barking dogs never bite. The danger in France arose from silent and instantaneous action. They said nothing, and did everything. Ours say everything, and will do nothing."

Threatened folk live long.

"Longer lives he that is threatened than he that is

---

[1] Apud Bactryanos vulgo usurpabant canem timidum vehementius latrare quam mordere.

[2] Was schadet das Hundes Bellen der nicht beisst?

[3] Cave tibi cane muto et aqua silente.

[4] Schweigender Hund beisst am ersten.

hanged" (Italian).[1] "More are threatened than are stabbed" (Spanish).[2] "Threatened folk, too, eat bread" (Portuguese).[3] "David did not slay Goliath with words" (Icelandic).[4] "No one dies of threats" (Dutch).[5] "Not all threateners fight" (Dutch).[6] "Some threaten who are afraid" (French).[7] "A curse does not knock an eye out unless the fist go with it" (Danish).[8] "The cat's curse hurts the mice less than her bite" (Livonian).

Lang mint, little dint. — Scotch.

That is, a blow long aimed or threatened has little force ; or, as the Italians and Spaniards say, "A blow threatened was never well given."[9]

Silence grips the mouse.

"A mewing cat was never a good mouser" (Spanish).[10] "He that threatens, warns" (German).[11] "He that threatens wastes his anger" (Portuguese).[12] "The threat-

---

[1] Vive più il minacciato che l'impiccato.
[2] Mas son los amenazados que los acuchillados.
[3] Tambem os ameaçados comem paō.
[4] Ekks Davith Goliat med ordum drap.
[5] Van dreigen sterft man niet.
[6] Alle dreigers vechten niet.
[7] Tel menace qui a peur.
[8] Bande bider ei Öie ud, uden Næven fölger med.
[9] Schiaffo minacciato, mai ben dato. Bofeton amagado, nunca bien dado.
[10] Gato maublador nunca buen caçador.
[11] Wer droht, warnt.
[12] Quem ameaça, su ira gasta.

ener loses the opportunity of vengeance" (Spanish).[1]
"Threats are arms for the threatened" (Italian).[2]

Fleying [frightening] a bird is no the way to grip it. — *Scotch.*
The way to catch a bird is no to fling your bonnet at her. — *Scotch.*

"Hares are not caught with beat of drum" (French).[3]

Let not your mousetrap smell of blood.
Never show your teeth when you can't bite.

Brag is a good dog, but Holdfast is a better.
A boaster and a liar are cousins german.

"Believe a boaster as you would a liar" (Italian).[4]
"Who is the greatest liar? He that talks most of himself" (Chinese).

The greatest talkers are always the least doers.
Great boast, small roast.

"Great vaunters, little doers" (French).[5] "It is not the hen which cackles most that lays most eggs" (Dutch).[6]
"A long tongue betokens a short hand" (Spanish).[7]

---

[1] El amenazador hace perder el lugar de venganza.
[2] Le minaccie son arme del minacciato.
[3] On ne prend pas le lèvre au tambour.
[4] Credi al vantatore come al mentitore.
[5] Grands vanteurs, petits faiseurs.
[6] Het hoen, dat het meest kakelt, geeft de meeste eijers niet.
[7] La lengua luenga es señal de mano corta

Saying gangs cheap. — *Scotch.*
Saying and doing are two things.

" From saying to doing is a long stretch " (French).[1]
" Words are female, deeds are male" (Italian).[2] " Words
will not do for my aunt, for she does not trust even
deeds " (Spanish).[3]

His wind shakes no corn. — *Scotch.*
Harry Chuck ne'er slew a man till he cam nigh him. — *Scotch.*

Harry Chuck is understood to have been a vaporing
fellow of the ancient Pistol order, one of those who would
give "a great stab to a dead Moor" (Spanish).[4] " It
is easy to frighten a bull from the window " (Italian).[5]
" Many are brave when the enemy flees " (Italian).[6]

It is well said, but who will bell the cat? — *Scotch.*

" The mice consult together how to take the cat, but
they do not agree upon the matter " (Livonian).   " Ar-
chibald Douglas, Earl of Angus, a man remarkable for
strength of body and mind, acquired the popular name
of Bell-the-Cat upon the following remarkable occasion :
When the Scottish nobility assembled to deliberate on

---

1 Du dire au fait il y a grand trait.
2 Le parole son femmine, e i fatti son maschi.
3 No son palabras para mi tia, que aun de las obras no se fia.
4 A moro muerto gran lanzada.
5 E facile far paura al toro dalla fenestra.
6 Molli son bravi quando l'inimico frigge.

putting the obnoxious favorites of James III. to death,
Lord Grey told them the fable of the mice, who re-
solved that one of their number should put a bell round
the neck of the cat, to warn them of its coming; but
no one was so hardy as to attempt it. 'I understand
the moral,' said Angus; 'I will bell the cat. He beard-
ed the king to purpose by hanging the favorites over the
bridge of Lauder; Cochran, their chief, being elevated
higher than the rest." — (*Note to Marmion.*)

> **Self-praise is no commendation.**
> **Self-praise stinks.**
> **Ye live beside ill-neebors.** — *Scotch.*
> **Your trumpeter is dead.**

The last two are taunts addressed to persons who sound
their own praises.

> **A man may love his house weel, and no ride on the riggen o' t.** —
> *Scotch.*

A man does not prove the depth and sincerity of his
sentiments by an ostentatious display of them.

> **Good wine needs no bush.**
> **Gude ale needs nae wisp.** — *Scotch.*

A bunch of twigs, or a wisp of hay or straw hung up
at a roadside house, is a sign that drink is sold within.
This custom, which still lingers in the cider-making counties of the west of England, and prevails more generally
in France, is derived from the Romans, among whom a
bunch of ivy, the plant sacred to Bacchus, was appro-
priately used as the sign of a wine-shop. They, too,

used to say, " Vendible wine needs no ivy hung up." [1]
" Good wine needs no crier" (Spanish). [2] " It sells itself"
(Spanish). [3] " Bosky" is one of the innumerable euphem-
isms for " drunk."   Probably the phrase, "he is bosky,"
originally conveyed an allusion to the symbolical use of
the bush, with which all good fellows were familiar in
the olden time.

---

[1] Vino vendibili suspensa hedera non est opus.
[2] El vino bueno no ha menester pregonero.
[3] El buen vino la venta trae consigo.

SECRETS.

No secrets but between two.

" Where could you have heard that ? " said a friend to Grattan. " Why, it is a profound secret." " I heard it," said Grattan, " where secrets are kept—in the street." Napoleon I. used to say, " Secrets travel fast in Paris." [1]

Three may keep counsel if two be away.

We are told in several languages that " The secret of two is God's secret — the secret of three is all the world's ; " [2] and the Spaniards hold that " What three know every creature knows." [3] The surest plan is, of course, not to trust to anybody ; and this was the plan pursued by Alva and by Q. Metellus Macedonicus, whose maxim, " If my tunic knew my secret I would burn it forthwith," has been turned by the French into a rhyming proverb of their own : " Let the shirt next your skin not know what 's within." [4] The Chinese say, " What is whispered in the ear is often heard a hundred

---

[1] Les confidences vont vite à Paris.

[2] Secret de deux, secret de Dieu ; secret de trois, secret de tous.

[3] Lo que saben tres, sabe toda res.

[4] Que ta chemise ne sache ta guise.

miles off." Truly, " Nothing is so burdensome as a secret " (French).[1] The Livonians have this humorous hyperbole, " Confide a secret to a dumb man and it will make him speak." King Midas's barber scraped a hole in the earth, and, lying down, poured into it the tremendous secret that oppressed him ; but the earth did not keep it close, for it sprouted up with the growing corn, which proclaimed, with articulate rustlings, " King Midas hath the ears of an ass."

Tom Noddy's secret.

Or, " The secret of Polichinelle " (French);[2] that is to say, one which is known to everybody. This is what the Spaniards call " The secret of Anchuelos."[3] The town of that name lies in a gorge between two steep hills, on one of which a shepherd tended his flock, on the other a shepherdess. This pair kept up an amorous converse by bawling from hill to hill, but always with many mutual injunctions of secrecy.

Murder will out.

" And a man's child cannot be hid," adds Lancelot Gobbo. The English proverb is used jocosely, though derived from an awful sense of the fatality, as it were, with which bloody secrets are almost always brought to light. It seems to us as though the order of nature were inverted when the perpetrator of a murder escapes de-

---

[1] Rien ne pèse tant qu'um secret.
[2] Le secret de Polichinelle.
[3] El secreto de Anchuelos.

tection. This faith in Nemesis was expressed in the ancient Greek proverb, " The cranes of Ibycus," of which this is the story : The lyric poet Ibycus was murdered by robbers on his way to Corinth, and with his last breath committed the task of avenging him to a flock of cranes, the only living things in sight besides himself and his murderers. The latter, some time after, sitting in the theatre at Corinth, saw a flock of cranes overhead, and one of them said, scoffingly, " Lo, there the avengers of Ibycus ! " These words were caught up by some near them, for already the poet's disappearance had excited alarm. The men being questioned, betrayed themselves, and were led to their doom, and " The cranes of Ibycus " passed into a proverb. This story may serve to show how

Daylight will peep through a small hole.

" Eggs are close things," say the Chinese, " but the chicks come out at last." " A secret fire is discovered by the smoke " (Catalan).[1]

To let the cat out of the bag.

To betray a secret inadvertently. I cannot tell what is the origin of this phrase. Can it be that it alludes to the practice of selling cats for hares ? A fraudulent vendor, while pressing a customer " to buy a cat in a bag " (see p. 58), might in an unguarded moment let him see enough to detect the imposition.

---

[1] For secreto, lo fumo lo descovre.

176 PROVERBS OF ALL NATIONS.

When rogues fall out honest men come by their own.

They peach upon each other. " Thieves quarrel, and thefts are discovered" (Spanish).[1] " Gossips fall out, and tell each other truths" (Spanish).[2] "When the cook and the butler fall out we shall know what is become of the butter" (Dutch).

Tell your secret to your servant, and you make him your master.

Juvenal notes the policy of the Greek adventurers in Rome to worm out the secrets of the house, and so make themselves feared. " To whom you tell your secret you surrender your freedom" (Spanish).[3] " Tell your friend your secret, and he will set his foot on your throat" (Spanish).[4]

Walls have ears.

" Hills see, walls hear" (Spanish).[5] " The forest has ears, the field has eyes" (German).[6]

What soberness conceals drunkenness reveals.

" What is in the heart of the sober man is on the tongue of the drunken man" (Latin).[7] " In wine

---

[1] Pelean los ladrones, y descubriense los hurtos.
[2] Riñen las comadres, y duense las verdades.
[3] A quien dices tu puridad, á ese das tu libertad.
[4] Di á tu amigo tu secreto, y tenerte ha el pie en el pescuezo.
[5] Montes veen, paredes oyen.
[6] Der Wald hat Ohren, das Feld hat Augen.
[7] Quod est in corde sobrii est in ore ebrii.

is truth " (Latin).[1] " Wine wears no breeches "
(Spanish).[2]

> When wine sinks, words swim.[3]
>
> When the wine is in the wit is out.

---

[1] In vino veritas.

[2] El vino anda sin calças.

[3] This is in Herodotus : Ὄινου κατίοντος ἔπιπλεουσιν ἐπῆ.

12

RETRIBUTION.—PENAL JUSTICE.

He that is born to be hanged will never be drowned.

The water will ne'er waur the woodie. — *Scotch.*

THAT is, the water will never defraud the gallows of its due. Gonzago, in *The Tempest*, says of the boatswain, " I have great comfort from this fellow : methinks he hath no drowning mark upon him ; his complexion is perfect gallows. Stand fast, good fate, to his hanging! Make the rope of his destiny our cable, for our own doth little advantage. If he be not born to be hanged our case is miserable."

The Danes say, " He that is to be hanged will never be drowned, unless the water goes over the gallows." [1] Such punctilious accuracy in fixing the limits of the proposition considerably enhances its grim humor. There is a fine touch of ghastly horror in its Dutch equivalent, — " What belongs to the raven does not drown." [2] The platform on which criminals were executed and gibbeted was called, in the picturesque language of the middle ages, the " ravenstone." " He

---

[1] Han drukner ikke som henge skal, uden Vandet gaaer over Galgen.

[2] Wat den raven toebehoort verdrinkt niet.

that is to die by the gallows may dance on the river"
(Italian).[1]

> " He 'll be hanged yet,
> Though every drop of water swear against it,
> And gape at wid'st to glut him."

Give a thief rope enough and he 'll hang himself.

Every fox must pay his own skin to the flayer.

**Air day or late day, the tod's [fox's] hide finds aye the flaying-
knife.** — *Scotch.*

In spite of all his cunning, the rogue will soon or late
come to a bad end. " Foxes find themselves at last at
the furrier's" (French).[2] " No mad dog runs seven
years " (Dutch).[3]

Hanging goes by hap.

If a man is hanged it is a sign that he was pre-
destined to that end. " The gallows was made for the
unlucky " (Spanish).[4] It is not always a man's fault so
much as his misfortune that he dies of a hempen fever.
As Captain Macheath sings :

> Since laws were made for every degree,
> To curb vice in others as well as in me,
> I wonder we ha'n't better company
> Upon Tyburn tree."

---

[1] Chi ha da morir di forca, può ballar sul fiume.

[2] Enfin les renards se trouvent chez le pelletier.

[3] Er liep geen dolle hond zeven jaar.

[4] Para los desdichados se hizo la horca.

But "Money does not get hanged" (German).[1] It sits on the judgment-seat, and sends poor rogues to the hulks or to Jack Ketch. As it was in the days of Diogenes the cynic, so it is now : " Great thieves hang petty thieves " (French);[2] and, whilst " Petty thieves are hanged, people take off their hats to great ones " (German).[3]

> First hang and draw,
> Then hear the cause by Lidford law.

Ray informs us that " Lidford is a little and poor but ancient corporation in Devonshire, with very large privileges, where a Court of Stannaries was formerly kept." The same sort of expeditious justice was practised in Scotland and in Spain, as testified by proverbs of both countries. At Peralvillo the Holy Brotherhood used to execute in this manner robbers taken in the fact, or " red-hand," as the Scotch forcibly expressed it. Hence the Spanish saying, " Peralvillo justice : after the man is hanged, try him."[4] The Scotch equivalent for this figures with dramatic effect in that scene of *The Fair Maid of Perth* where Black Douglas has just discovered the murder of the Prince of Rothsay, and exclaims —

" 'Away with the murderers! hang them over the battlements !'

---

[1] Geld wird nicht gehenkt.

[2] Les grands voleurs font pendre les petits.

[3] Kleine Diebe henkt man, vor grossen zieht man den Hut ab.

[4] La justicia de Peralvillo, que ahorcado el hombre le hace la perquisa.

" ' But, my lord, some trial may be fitting,' answered Balveny.

" ' To what purpose?' answered Douglas. 'I have taken them red-hand; my authority will stretch to instant execution. Yet stay: have we not some Jedwood men in our troop?'

" ' Plenty of Turnbulls, Rutherfords, Ainslies, and so forth,' said Balveny.

" ' Call me an inquest of these together; they are all good men and true, save a little shifting for their living. Do you see to the execution of these felons, while I hold a court in the great hall, and we'll try whether the jury or the provost-marshal shall do their work first: we will have

Jedwood justice — hang in haste, and try at leisure.' "

He that invented the "maiden" first hanselled it. — *Scotch.*

This was the Regent Morton, who was the first man beheaded by an instrument of his own invention, called the "maiden." His enemies thought it was

"Sport
To see the engineer hoist by his own petard; "

and even those who pitied him felt that "no law was juster than that the artificers of death should perish by their own art."[1]

---

[1] Nec lex est justior ulla
Quam necis artifices arte perire sua.

If he has no gear to tine, he has shins to pine. — *Scotch.*

That is, if he has not wealth to lose, or means to pay a fine, he must be clapped in the stocks or in fetters. " He that has no money must pay with his skin " (German).[1] " Where there is no money there is no forgiveness of sins " (German).[2]

---

[1] Wer kein Geld hat, mussmit der Haut bezahlen.
[2] Wo kein Geld ist, da ist auch keine Vergebung der Sünden.

WEALTH.—POVERTY.—PLENTY.—
WANT.

Happy is the son whose father went to the devil.

On the other hand, the Portuguese say, " Alas for the son whose father goes to heaven ! " [1] the presumption being that a man does not go that way whilst amassing great wealth; for " He that is afraid of the devil does not grow rich " (Italian). [2] " To do so one has only to turn one's back on God " (French). [3] Audley, a noted lawyer and usurer in the reigns of James I. and Charles I., was asked what might be the value of his newly-obtained office in the Court of Wards. He replied, " It may be worth some thousands of pounds to him who after his death would instantly go to heaven ; twice as much to him who would go to purgatory ; and nobody knows how much to him who would adventure to go to hell." Audley's biographer hints that he did adventure that way for the four hundred thousand pounds he left behind him at his departure. " The river does not

---

[1] Guay do filho que o pai vai a paraiso.

[2] Chi ha paura del diavolo non fa roba.

[3] Il ne faut que tourner le dos à Dieu pour devenir riche.

become swollen with clear water" (Italian).[1] According to a Latin proverb, quoted with approval by St. Jerome, "A rich man is either a rogue or a rogue's heir."[2] "To be rich, one must have a relation at home with the devil" (Italian).[3] "Gold goes to the Moor;" that is, to the man without a conscience (Portuguese).[4]

"The poets feign," says Bacon, "that when Plutus, which is riches, is sent from Jupiter, he limps and goes slowly; but when he is sent from Pluto he runs and is swift of foot: meaning that riches gotten by good means and just labor pace slowly, but when they come by the death of others (as by the course of inheritance, testaments, and the like), they come tumbling upon a man. But it might be applied likewise to Pluto, taking him for the devil; for when riches come from the devil (as by fraud and oppression and unjust means) they come upon speed. The ways to enrich are many, and most of them foul."

"He that maketh haste to be rich shall not be innocent" (Proverbs xxviii. 22). "Who would be rich in a year gets hanged in half a year" (Spanish).[5]

> Plenty makes dainty.[6]
> As the sow fills the draught sours.
> Hunger is the best sauce.

---

[1] Il fiume non s'ingrossa d'acqua chiara.
[2] Dives aut iniquus aut iniqui hæres.
[3] Por esser riceo bisogna avere un parente a casa al diavolo.
[4] Vaise o ouro ao mouro.
[5] Quien en un año quiere ser rico, al medio le ahorcan.
[6] Abondance engendre fàcherie.

" Hunger makes raw beans sweet" (German).
" Hunger is the best cook" (German). " The full
stomach loatheth the honeycomb, but to the hungry
every bitter thing is sweet" (Proverbs). " Brackish
water is sweet in a dry land" (Portuguese).[1]

> A hungry horse makes a clean manger.
> Hungry dogs will eat dirty puddings.
> A hungry man sees far.

" A hungry man discovers more than a hundred lawyers" (Spanish).[2] Want sharpens industry and invention. " He thinks of everything who wants bread"
(French).[3] " A poor man is all schemes" (Spanish).[4]

> " Largitor artium, ingeniique magister
>   Venter."

" Poverty and hunger have many learned disciples"
(German).[5] " Poverty is the sixth sense."[6] " It is
cunning : it catches even a fox" (German).[7]

> Need makes the old wife trot.[8]
> Need makes the naked man run.
> Need makes the naked quean spin.

---

[1] Agoa salobra na terra seca he doce.
[2] Mas descubre un hambriento que cien letrados.
[3] De tout s'avise à qui pain faut.
[4] Hombre pobre todo es trazas.
[5] Armuth und Hunger haben viel gelehrte Jünger.
[6] Armuth ist der sechste Sinn.
[7] Armuth ist listig, sie fängt auch einen Fuchs.
[8] The same in Italian, Bisogna fa trottar la vecchia; and in
French, Besoin fait vieille trotter.

" Hunger sets the dog a-hunting " (Italian).[1] " Hunger drives the wolf out of the wood " (Italian).[2]

Hunger will break through stone walls.

" A hungry dog fears not the stick " (Italian) ;[3] whereas, " The full-fed sheep is frightened at her own tail " (Spanish).[4]

Poverty parteth good fellowship.

An old Scotch song says :

> " When I hae saxpence under my thumb,
>   Then I get credit in ilka town ;
>   But when I hae naething they bid me gang by :
>   Hech ! poverty parts good company."

Poverty is no crime.

Some say it is worse. " Poverty is no vice, but it is a sort of leprosy " (French).[5]

---

[1] La forame il can per fame.
[2] La fame caccia il lupo fuor del bosco.
[3] Can affamato non ha paura del bastone.
[4] Carnero harto de su rabo se espanta.
[5] Pauvreté n'est pas vice, mais c'est une espèce de laiderie.

BEGINNING AND END.

A good beginning makes a good ending.
Well begun is half done.

TERSELY translated from the Latin, *Dimidium facti
qui bene cœpit habet.* "A beard lathered is half shaved,"
say the Spaniards.[1] In an article on the "Philosophy
of Proverbs," the author of the "Curiosities of Literature" gives an example from the Italian, which he
deems of peculiar interest, "for it is perpetuated by
Dante, and is connected with the character of Milton."
Besides these distinctions, it has a third (not surmised
by Disraeli), as a linguistic curiosity; for though it con-
sists of but four words, and those among the commonest
in the language, its literal meaning is undetermined, and
diametrically opposite interpretations have been given
of it even by native authorities. *Cosa fatta capo ha* is
the proverb in question, which some understand as sig-
nifying, "A deed done has an end;" or, as the Scotch
say, "A thing done is no to do." It is thus rendered
by Torriano in 1666; whilst Giusti, in 1853, explains
it as meaning, "A deed done has a beginning;" or, in
other words, if you would accomplish anything, you

---

[1] Barba remojada, medio rapada.

must not content yourself with pondering over it forever, but must proceed to action. Such another instance of divided opinion respecting the import of four familiar words in a simply-constructed sentence is probably not to be found in the history of modern languages.

This proverb is the "bad word" to which tradition ascribes the origin of the civil wars that long desolated Tuscany. When Buondelmonte broke his engagement with a lady of the Amadei family, and married another, the kinsmen of the injured lady assembled to consider how they should deal with the offender. They inclined to pass sentence of death upon him; but their fear of the evils that might ensue from that decision long held them in suspense. At last Mosca Lamberti cried out that "those who talk of many things effect nothing," quoting, says Macchiavelli, "that trite and common adage, *Cosa fatta capo ha.*" This decided the question. Buondelmonte was murdered; and the deed immediately involved Florence in those miserable conflicts of Guelphs and Ghibellines, from which she had stood aloof until then. The "bad word" uttered by Mosca has been immortalized by Dante (*Inferno*, xxviii.), and variously rendered by his English translators. Cary presents the passage thus:

> " Then one
> Maimed of each hand uplifted in the gloom
> The bleeding stumps, that they with gory spots
> Sullied his face, and cried, 'Remember thee
> Of Mosca too — I who, alas! exclaimed,
> The deed once done, there is an end — that proved
> A seed of sorrow to the Tuscan race.' "

Wright's version is:

> " Then one deprived of both his hands, who stood
> Lifting the bleeding stumps amid the dim
> Dense air, so that his face was stained with blood,
> Cried, ' In thy mind let Mosca bear a place,
> Who said, alas ! Deed done is well begun —
> Words fraught with evil to the Tuscan race.' "

Disraeli adopts Cary's interpretation of the proverb, and does not seem to suspect that it can have any other. Milton appears to have used it in the same sense. " When deeply engaged," says Disraeli, " in writing ' The Defence of the People,' and warned that it might terminate in his blindness, he resolutely concluded his work, exclaiming with great magnanimity, although the fatal prognostication had been accomplished, *Cosa fatta capo ha!* Did this proverb also influence his decision on that great national event, when the most honest-minded fluctuated between doubts and fears ? "

The first blow is half the battle.

It is as good as two, according to the Italians.

The hardest step is over the threshold.

" The first step is all the difficulty "(French).[1] It is well known that after St. Dennis was decapitated he picked up his head, and walked a league with it in his hand to the spot where his church was afterwards erected. Recounting this miracle one day in a private circle, Cardinal de Polignac laid great stress on the

---

[1] Ce n'est que le premier pas qui coûte.

length of the way traversed in that manner by the mar-
tyred saint; whereupon Madame du Deffaut remarked
that this was not the most surprising part of the miracle,
for in such cases " the first step was all the difficulty."

Everything has a beginning.

A child must creep ere it can go.

" Every beginning is feeble" (Latin).[1]   " ' Every
beginning is hard,' as the thief said when he began by
stealing an anvil" (German).[2]

Rome was not built in a day.

---

[1] Omne principium est debile.

[2] Aller Anfang ist schwer, sprach der Dieb, und stahl zuerst
einen Ambos.

OFFICE.

The office shows the man.
'T is the place shows the man.

IT tries his capacity, and shows what stuff he is made of. But it also forms the man; it teaches him (German)[1] if he has the faculty to be taught, so that it may be said with some truth, " To whom God gives an office he gives understanding also" (German).[2] " A great place strangely qualifies," saith Selden. " John Read was groom of the chamber to my lord of Kent. Attorney-General Roy being dead, some were saying, how would the king do for a fit man? 'Why, any man,' says John Read, 'may execute the place.' 'I warrant,' says my lord, 'thou thinkest thou understand'st enough to perform it.' 'Yes,' quoth John; 'let the king make me attorney, and I would fain see that man that durst tell me there's anything I understand not.'" The proverb at the head of this paragraph is literally translated from a Greek maxim, attributed by Sophocles to Solon, and to Bias by Aristotle.

---

[1] Das Amt lehrt den Mann.

[2] Wein Gott ein Amt giebt, dem giebt er auch Verstand.

He is a poor cook that cannot lick his own fingers.

And " He is a bad manager of honey" who does not
help himself in the same way (French).[1] The rule
applies to all who have the fingering of good things,
whether in a public or a private capacity. " He who
manages other people's wealth does not go supperless
to bed" (Italian).[2] "All offices are greasy" (Dutch).[3]
Something sticks to them. Wheels are greased to make
them run smoothly, and in some countries it is found
that what the Dutch call smear money may be applied
to official palms with advantage to the operator. The
French call this *Graisser la patte à quelqu'un.* " ' Hast
thou no money ? then turn placeman,' said the court fool
to his sovereign'" (German).[4] King James, we are
told by L'Estrange, was once complaining of the lean-
ness of his hunting-horse. Archie, his fool, standing by,
said to him, "If that be all, take no care ; I 'll teach
your Majesty a way to raise his flesh presently ; and if
he be not as fat as ever he can wallow, you shall ride
me." "I prithee, fool, how ?" said the king. "Why,
do but make him a bishop, and I 'll warrant you," says
Archie.

A good deal of surreptitious finger-licking and fatten-
ing would be prevented if this truth were clearly under-

---

[1] Celui gouverne bien mal le miel, qui n'en taste et ses doigts
n'en lesche.

[2] Chi maneggia quel degli altri, non va a letto senza cena.

[3] Alle amten zijn smeerig.

[4] Hast du kein Geld ? so wird ein Amtmann, sagte jeuer Hof-
narr zu seinen Fürsten.

stood, that "Office without pay [or with inadequate pay] makes thieves" (German).[1] "He cannot keep a good course who serves without reward" (Italian).[2]

A man gets little thanks for losing his own.

An excuse for taking the perquisites of office, however extortionate they may be.

It is the clerk that makes the justice.

The magistrate would often be wrong in his law if he were not kept right by the clerk. "The blood of the soldier makes the captain great" (Italian).[3]

For faut o' wise men fules sit on binks [benches]. — Scotch.

"For want of good men they made my father alcalde" (Spanish).[4] We do not always see the right man in the right place.

Never deal with the man when you can deal with the master.

"It is better to have to do with God than with his saints"[5] is a French proverb, which Voltaire has fitted with a droll story. A king of Spain, he tells us, had promised to bestow relief upon the people of the country round Burgos, who had been ruined by war. They

---

[1] Amt ohne Sold macht Diebe.

[2] Buona via non può tenere
Quel chi serve senz' avere.

[3] Il sangue dei soldati fa grande il capitano.

[4] Por falta de hombres buenos, á mi padre hicieron alcalde.

[5] Il vaut mieux avoir affaire à Dieu qu'à ses saints.

13

flocked to the palace, but the doorkeepers would not let them in except on condition of having part of what they should get. Having consented to this, the countrymen entered the royal hall, where their leader knelt at the monarch's feet, and said, " I beseech your Royal Highness to command that every man of us here shall receive a hundred lashes." " An odd petition, truly ! " said the king. " Why do you ask for such a thing ? " " Because," said the peasant, "your people insist on having the half of whatever you give us."

M. Quitard believes that the saints referred to in the French proverb are the " frost " or " vintage saints," [1] so called because their festivals, which occur in April, are noted in the popular calendar as days on which frost is injurious to the young green crops and to vines. The husbandmen, whose fields and vineyards were injured by the inclemency of the weather, used to hold these saints responsible for the damage they ought to have prevented, and the reproaches addressed to them might very naturally take the form perpetuated in the proverb. This is the more probable as it is recorded in the ecclesiastical annals of Cahors and Rhodez that the angry agriculturists were in the habit of flogging the images of the frost saints, defacing their pictures, and otherwise maltreating them. Rabelais asserts, with mock gravity, that, in order to put an end to these scandalous irregularities, a bishop of Auxerre proposed to transfer the festivals of the frost saints to the dog days, and make the month of August change place with April.

---

[1] Saints gélifs, saints vendangeurs.

A king's cheese goes half away in parings.

His revenues are half eaten up before they enter his coffers. Before Sully took the French finances in hand, such was the system of plunder established by the farmers of the revenue, that the state realized only one-fifth of the gross amount of taxes imposed on the subjects; the other four-fifths were consumed by the financiers. Under such a wasteful system as this, or one in any degree like it, one might well say that

King's chaff is worth other men's corn.

The perquisites belonging to the king's service are better than the wages earned elsewhere.

The clerk wishes the priest to have a fat dish. —*Gaelic.*

LAW AND LAWYERS.

Law-makers should not be law-breakers.

PARLIAMENT has made it penal to pollute the air of towns with smoke, and the *Builder* complains that more smoke issues from Parliament's own chimneys than from any six factories in London.

Abundance of law breaks no law.

It is safer to exceed than to fall short of what the law requires.

In a thousand pounds of law there is not an ounce of love.

A pennyweight of love is worth a pound weight of law.

So much more cogent is the one than the other.

Laws were made for rogues.

"For the upright there are no laws" (German).[1] They are designed to control those to whom it may be said —

Ye wad do little for God if the deil were dead. — *Scotch.*

"The fear o' hell 's a hangman's whip
    To keep the wretch in order;
But where ye feel your honor grip,
    Let that be aye your border.

---

[1] Für Gerechte giebt es keine Gesetze.

" Its slightest touches, instant pause,
Debar a' side pretences,
And resolutely keep its laws,
Uncaring consequences."

He that loves law will get his fill of it.
Agree, for the law is costly.
Law 's costly; tak a pint and 'gree. — *Scotch.*

Lord Mansfield declared that if any man claimed a
field from him, he would give it up, provided the conces-
sion were kept secret, rather than engage in proceedings
at law. Hesiod, in admonishing his brother always to
prefer a friendly accommodation to a lawsuit, gave to
the world the paradoxical proverb, " The half is more
than the whole." Very often " A lean agreement is
better than a fat lawsuit" (Italian).[1] " Lawyers' garments are lined with suitors' obstinacy" (Italian) ;[2] and
" Their houses are built of fools' heads" (French).[3]
Doctors and lawyers are notoriously shy of taking what
they prescribe for others. " No good lawyer ever goes
to law" (Italian).[4] Lord Chancellor Thurlow did so
once, but in his case the exception approved the rule.
A house had been built for him by contract, but he had
made himself liable for more than the stipulated price
by ordering some departures from the specification whilst
the work was in progress. He refused to pay the ad-
ditional charge ; the builder brought an action and got a

---

[1] E meglio un magro accordo che una grassa lite.
[2] Le vesti degli avvocati son fodrate dell' ostinazion dei litiganti.
[3] Les maisons des avocats sont faictes de la teste des folz.
[4] Nessum buon avvocato piatisce mai.

verdict against him, and surly Thurlow never afterwards set foot within the house which was the monument of his wrong-headedness and its chastisement.

Refer my coat, and lose a sleeve. — *Scotch.*

Arbitrators generally make both parties abate something of their pretensions.

Fair and softly, as lawyers go to heaven.

The odds are great against their ever getting there, if it be true that " Unless hell is full, never will a lawyer be saved" (French).[1] " The greater lawyer, the worse Christian" (Dutch).[2] " ' Virtue in the middle,' said the devil, as he sat between two attorneys " (Danish).[3]

---

[1] Si enfer n'est plein, oncques n'y aura d'avocat sauvé.

[2] Hoe grooter jurist, hoe boozer Christ.

[3] Dyden i Midten, sagde Fanden, han sal imellem to Procuratoren.

PHYSIC.—PHYSICIANS.—MAXIMS RELATING TO HEALTH.

If the doctor cures, the sun sees it; if he kills, the earth hides it.

" THE earth covers the mistakes of the physician" (Italian, Spanish).[1] " Bleed him and purge him; if he dies, bury him (Spanish).[2] It is a melancholy truth that " The doctor is often more to be feared than the disease" (French).[3] " Throw physic to the dogs," is in effect the advice given by many eminent physicians, and by some of the greatest thinkers the world has seen. " Shun doctors and doctors' drugs if you wish to be well,"[4] was the seventh, last, and best rule of health laid down by the famous physician Hoffmann. Sir William Hamilton declared that " Medicine in the hands in which it is vulgarly dispensed is a curse to humanity rather than a blessing;" and Sir Astley Cooper did not scruple to avow that " The science of medicine was founded on conjecture and improved by murder. It is a remark-

---

[1] Gli errori del medico gli copre la terra. Los yerros del médico la tierra los cubre.

[2] Sungrarle y purgarle; si se muriere, enterrarle.

[3] Le médecin est souvent plus à craindre que la maladie.

[4] Fuge medicos ac medicamenta, si vis esse salvus.

able fact that " The doctor seldom takes physic" (Italian).[1] He does not appear to have a very lively faith in his own art. As for his alleged cures, their reality does not pass unquestioned. It is true that " Dear physic always does good, if not to the patient, at least to the apothecary" (German) ;[2] but " It is God that cures, and the doctor gets the money" (Spanish).[3] Save your money, then, and " If you have a friend who is a doctor, take off your hat to him, and send him to the house of your enemy" (Spanish).[4]

The best physicians are Dr. Diet, Dr. Quiet, and Dr. Merriman.
Every man at forty is either a fool or a physician.
A creaking gate hangs long on its hinges.

Valetudinarians often outlive persons of robust constitution who take less care of themselves. A French saying to this purpose, which is too idiomatic to be translated, was neatly applied by Pozzo di Borgo in a conversation with Lady Holland. Her ladyship, exulting in the duration of the Whig government, notwithstanding the prevalent anticipations of their fall, said to him : " Vous voyez, Monsieur l'Ambassadeur, que nous vivons toujours." " Oui, madame," he replied, " les petites santés durent quelquefois longtemps." " Creak-

---

[1] Di rado il medico piglia medicina.

[2] Theure Arznei hilft immer, wenn nicht dem Kranken doch dem Apotheker.

[3] Dios es el que sana, y el medico lleva la plata.

[4] Si tienes medico amigo, quitale la gorra, y envialo á casa de tu enemigo.

ing carts last longest" (Dutch).[1] "The flawed pots are
the most lasting" (French).[2]

A groaning wife and a grunting horse ne'er failed their master.

> Seek your salve where ye got your sore. — *Scotch.*
> Take a hair of the dog that bit you.

Advice given to persons suffering the after-pains of a
carouse. The same stimulant which caused their ner-
vous depression will also relieve it. The metaphor is
derived from an old medical practice to which Seneca
makes some allusion, and which is commended in a
rhyming French adage to this effect: " With the hair of
the beast that bit thee, or with its blood, thou wilt be
cured."[3] Cervantes, in his tale of *La Gitanilla*, thus
describes an old gypsy woman's manner of treating a
person bitten by a dog : — " She took some of the dog's
hairs, fried them in oil, and after washing with wine the
two bites she found on the patient's left leg, she put
the hairs and the oil upon them, and over this dress-
ing a little chewed green rosemary. She then bound
the leg up carefully with clean bandages, made the
sign of the cross over it, and said, 'Now go to sleep,
friend, and with the help of God your hurts will not
signify.' "

---

[1] Krakende wagens duirren het langst.
[2] Les pots fêlés sont ceux qui durent le plus.
[3] Du poil de la bête qui te mordit,
Ou de son sang, seras guéri.

One nail drives out another.

This is the doctrine of homœopathy. " Poison quells poison " (Italian).[1]

" Tut, man ! one fire burns out another's burning,
    One pain is lessened by another's anguish.
Turn giddy, and be holp by backward turning :
    One desperate grief cures with another's languish.
Take thou some new infection to thine eye,
And the rank poison of the old will die."
— *Romeo and Juliet.*

**If the wind strike thee through a hole,
Go make thy will and mend thy soul.**

" A blast from a window is a shot from a crossbow " (Italian).[2]   " To a bull and a draught of air give way " (Spanish).[3]

One hour's sleep before midnight is worth two hours after it.

Ladies rightly call sleep before midnight " beauty sleep."

Old young, and old long.[4]

You must leave off the irregularities of youth betimes, if you wish to enjoy a long and hale old age ; for

Young men's knocks old men feel.

---

[1] Il veleno si spegne col veleno.
[2] Aria di fenestra, colpodi balestra.
[3] Al toro y al aire darles calle.
[4] Mature fias senex, si diu velis esse senex.

"The sins of our youth we atone for in our old age" (Latin).[1]

Rub your sore eye with your elbow.

He who laid down this rule of sound surgery was a man *qui ne se mouchait pas du talon;* he did not blow his nose with his heel. If a speck of dust enters your eye, close the lid gently, keep your fingers away from it, and leave the foreign body to be washed by the tears to the inner corner of the eye, whence it may be removed without difficulty.

---

[1] Quæ peccavimus juvenes, ea luimus senes.

CLERGY.

It's kittle shooting at corbies and clergy. — *Scotch.*

CROWS are very wary, and the clergy are vindictive; therefore it is ticklish work trying to get the better of either. " One must either not meddle with priests, or else smite them dead," say the Germans ;[1] and Huss, the Bohemian reformer, in denouncing the sins of the clergy in his day, has preserved for us a similar proverb of his countrymen : " If you have offended a clerk, kill him, else you will never have peace with him."[2] " The bites of priests and wolves are hard to heal " (German).[3] " Priests and women never forget " (German).[4] " How dangerous it was," says Gross, " to injure the meanest retainer of a religious house, is very ludicrously but justly expressed in the following old English adage, which I have somewhere met with :

---

[1] Man muss mit Pfaffen nicht anfangen, oder sie todtschlagen.

[2] Malum proverbium contra nos confinxerunt, dicentes, " Si offenderis clericum, interfice eum ; alias nunquam habebis pacem cum illo."

[3] Was Pfaffen beissen und Wölfe ist schwer zu heilen.

[4] Pfaffen und Weiber vergessen nie.

'Yf perchaunce one offend a freere's dogge, streight clameth the whole brotherhood, An heresy! An heresy!'"

There is an old German proverb to the same purpose, which Eiserlein heard once from the lips of an aged lay servitor of a monastery in the Black Forest: " Offend one monk, and the lappets of all cowls will flutter as far as Rome." [1]

What was good the friar never loved.

Popular opinion attributes to the clergy, both secular and regular, a lively regard for the good things of this life, and a determination to have their full share of them. " No priest ever died of hunger," is a remark made by the Livonians ; and they add, " Give the priests all thou hast, and thou wilt have given them nearly enough." " A priest's pocket is hard to fill," [2] at least in Denmark ; and the Italians say that " Priests, monks, nuns, and poultry never have enough." [3] "Abbot of Carzuela," cries the Spaniard, "you eat up the stew, and you ask for the stewpan." [4] The worst testimony against the monastic order comes from the countries in which they most abound: " Where friars swarm, keep your eyes open " (Spanish).[5] " Have neither a good monk for a friend, nor a bad one for an enemy" (Spanish).[6] "As

---

[1] Beleidigestu einen Münch, so knappe alle Kuttenzipfel bis nach Rom.

[2] Præstesæk er ond at fylde.

[3] Preti, frati, monache, e polli non si trovan mai satolli.

[4] Abad de Carçuela, comistes la olla, pedis la cacuela.

[5] Frailes sobrand', ojo alerte.

[6] Ni buen fraile por amigo, ni malo por enemigo.

for friars, live with them, eat with them, walk with them, and then sell them, for thus they do themselves " (Spanish).[1] The propensity of churchmen to identify their own personal interests with the welfare of the church is glanced at in the following : — " The monk that begs for God's sake begs for two " (Spanish, French).[2] "' Oh, what we must suffer for the church of God!' cried the abbot, when the roast fowl burned his fingers " (German).[3]

There's no mischief done in the world but there's a woman or a priest at the bottom of it.

---

[1] Frailes, vivĕr con ellos, y comer con ellos, y andar con ellos, y luego vender ellos, que asé hacen ellos.

[2] Fraile que pide por Dios, pide bor dos. Moine qui demande pour Dieu, demande pour deux.

[3] O was müssen wir der Kirche Gottes halber leiden ! rief der Abt, als ihm das gebratene Huhn die Finger versengt.

SEASONS.—WEATHER.

If the grass grow in Janiveer,
It grows the worse for it all the year.

"WHEN gnats dance in January the husbandman becomes a beggar" (Dutch).[1] An exception to these rules is recorded by Ray, who says that "in the year 1667 the winter was so mild that the pastures were very green in January ; yet was there scarcely ever known a more plentiful crop of hay than the summer following."

February fill dike, be it black or be it white.

All the months in the year curse a fair Februeer.

The hind had as lief see his wife on the bier
As that Candlemas day should be pleasant and clear.

Candlemas day is the 2d of February, when the Romish Church celebrates the purification of the Virgin Mary. On that day, also, the church candles are blessed for the whole year, and they are carried in procession in the hands of the faithful. Then the use of tapers at vespers and litanies, which prevails throughout the

---

[1] Als de muggen in Januar danssen, wordt de boer een bedelaar.

winter, ceases until the ensuing Allhallowmas: hence
the proverb —

> Cn Candlemas day
> Throw candle and candlestick away.

Browne, in his "Vulgar Errors," says there is a
general tradition in most parts of Europe that inferreth
the coldness of the succeeding winter from the shining of
the sun on Candlemas day, according to the proverbial
distich:

> *Si sol splendescat Maria purificante,*
> *Major erit glacies post festum quam fuit ante.*

> " If Candlemas day be fair and bright,
>   Winter will have another flight;
>   If on Candlemas day there be shower and rain,
>   Winter is gone, and will not come again."

Another version of this proverb current in the north
of England is —

> " If Candlemas day be dry and fair,
>   The half of winter's to come and mair;
>   If Candlemas day be wet and foul [pronounced *fool*],
>   The half of winter's gone to Yule."

March comes in like a lion and goes out like a lamb.

March comes in with adder heads and goes out with peacock tails.
> *— Scotch.*

A peck of March dust is worth a king's ransom.

A dry March never begs its bread.

A peck of March dust and a shower in May
Make the corn green and the fields gay.

March winds and April showers
Bring forth May flowers.

> March wind and May sun
> Make clothes white and maids dun.

> So many mists in March you see,
> So many frosts in May will be.

> March grass never did good.

" When gnats dance in March it brings death to sheep" (Dutch).[1]

> When April blows his horn it's good both for hay and corn.

" That is," says Ray, " when it thunders in April, for thunder is usually accompanied with rain."

> A cold April the barn will fill.
> April and May are the keys of the year.
> A May flood never did good.

This applies to England. In Spain and Italy they say, " Water in May is bread for all the year." [2]

> To wed in May is to wed poverty.

There were fewer marriages in Scotland in May, 1857, than in any other month of the year: it is an " unlucky month." The proverb is recorded by Washington Irving.

> A swarm of bees in May is worth a load of hay,
> A swarm in June is worth a silver spoon,
> But a swarm in July is not worth a fly.

> A shower in July, when the corn begins to fill,
> Is worth a plough of oxen and all belongs theretill.

---

[1] Als de muggen in Maart danssen, dat doet het schaap den dood aan.

[2] Acqua di Maggio, pane per tutto l'anno.

14

A dry summer never made a dear peck.

Drought never bred dearth in England.

The same thing, and no more, is meant by the following enigmatical rhyme:

" When the sand doth feed the clay,
England woe and well-a-day ;
But when the clay doth feed the sand,
Then is it well with old England."

The first of these two contingencies occurs after a wet summer — the second after a dry one ; and, as there is more clay than sand in England, there is a better harvest in the second case than in the first.

Dry August and warm doth harvest no harm.

They think differently on this point in the south of Europe. "A wet August never brings dearth" (Italian).[1] "When it rains in August it rains honey and wine " (Spanish).[2]

September blow soft till the fruit 's in the loft.

November take flail, let ships no more sail.

A green Christmas makes a fat churchyard.

It is a popular notion that a mild winter is less healthy than a frosty one ; but the Registrar-General's returns prove that it is quite the contrary. The mortality of the winter months is always in proportion to the intensity of the cold. The proverb, therefore, must

[1] Agosto humido non mena mai carestia.

[2] Quando llueve en Agosto, llueve miel y mosto.

be given up as a fallacy. There is some truth in this of the Germans, " A green Christmas, a white Easter." The probability is that a very mild winter will be followed by an inclement spring.

A snow year, a rich year.

Under water, dearth ; under snow, bread.

Winter's thunder and summer's flood
Never boded an Englishman good.

NATIONAL AND LOCAL CHARACTER-ISTICS.—LOCAL ALLUSIONS.

A right Englishman knows not when a thing is well.

It would seem, too, that he does not know when a thing is ill; for the French say the English were beaten at Waterloo, but had not the wit to know it.

A Scotsman is aye wise ahint the hand. — *Scotch.*

A Scotsman aye taks his mark frae a mischief. — *Scotch.*

Scotsmen reckon aye frae an ill hour. — *Scotch.*

That is, they always date from some untoward event. "A Scottish man," says James Kelly, "solicited the Prince of Orange to be made an ensign, for he had been a sergeant ever since his Highness ran away from Groll."

The Englishman weeps, the Irishman sleeps, but the Scotsman gaes till he gets it. — *Scotch.*

Such, according to Scotch report, is the conduct of the three when they want food.

The Welshman keeps nothing till he has lost it. — *Welsh.*

The older the Welshman, the more madman. — *Welsh.*

As long as a Welsh pedigree.

The Italianised Englishman is a devil incarnate. — *Italian*.[1]

This is the testimony of Italians. Of our country they say —

England is the paradise of women, the purgatory of purses, and the hell of horses. — *Italian*.[2]

War with all the world, and peace with England. — *Spanish*.[3]

Beware of a white Spaniard and of a swarthy Englishman. — *Dutch*.[4]

Apparently because they are out of kind, and therefore presumed to be uncanny.

He has more to do than the ovens of London at Christmas. — *Italian*.

They agree like the clocks of London. — *French, Italian*.

Which clocks disagree to this day. (*See Household Words*, No. 410.) " The city time measurers are so far behind each other that the last chime of eight has hardly fallen on the ear from the last church, when another sprightly clock is heard to begin the hour of nine. Each clock, however, governs, and is believed in by its own immediate neighborhood."

Shake a bridle over a Yorkshireman's grave, and he will rise and steal a horse.

He is Yorkshire.

He is a keen blade. " He's of Spoleto " (*E. Spoletino*), say the Italians.

---

[1] L'Inglese italianizzato, un diavolo incarnato.

[2] Inghilterra paradiso di donne, purgatorio di borse, e inferno di cavalli.

[3] Con todo el mondo guerra, y paz con Inglaterra.

[4] Op een witten Spanjaard en op een zwarten Engelschman moet men acht geven.

The devil will not come into Cornwall for fear of being put into a pie.

Cornish housewives make pies of such unlikely materials as potatoes, pilchards, etc.

> By Tre, Pol, and Pen,
> You shall know the Cornish men.

Surnames beginning with these syllables — *e. g.*, Tre lawney, Polwhele, Penrose — are originally Cornish.

A Scottish man and a Newcastle grindstone travel all the world over.

Newcastle grindstones were long reputed the best of their kind. Another version of the proverb associates them with rats and red herrings, things which are very widely diffused over the globe, but not more so than Scotchmen.

Three great evils come out of the north — a cold wind, a cunning knave, and a shrinking cloth.

He 's an Aberdeen's man ; he may take his word again. — *Scotch.*

An Aberdeen's man ne'er stands to the word that hurts him. —*Scotch.*

The people of Normandy labor under the same imputation : " A Norman has his say and his unsay." [1] This proverb is said to have arisen out of the ancient custom of the province, according to which contracts did not become valid until twenty-four hours after they had been signed, and either party was at liberty to retract during that interval.

---

[1] Un Normand a son dit et son dédit.

Wise men of Gotham.

Gotham is a village in Nottinghamshire, declared by universal consent, for reasons unknown, to be the head-quarters of stupidity in this country, on whose inhabitants all sorts of ridiculous stories might he fathered. The convenience of having such a butt for sarcasm has been recognized by all nations. The ancient Greeks had their Bœotia, which was for them what Swabia is for the modern Germans. The Italians compare foolish people to those of Zago, " who sowed needles that they might have a crop of crowbars, and dunged the steeple to make it grow." [1] The French say, " Ninety-nine sheep and a Champenese make a round hundred," [2] the man being a stupid animal like the rest. The Abbé· Tuet traces back the origin of this story to Cæsar's conquest of Gaul Before that period the wealth of Champagne consisted in flocks of sheep, which paid a rate in kind to the public revenue. The conqueror, wishing to favor the staple of the province, exempted from taxation all flocks numbering less than a hundred head, and the consequence was that the Champenese always divided their sheep into flocks of ninety-nine. But Cæsar was soon even with them, for he ordered that in future the shepherd of every flock should be counted as a sheep, and pay as one.

---

[1] Più pazzi di quei da Zago, che seminavano gucchie per raccogher poi pali di ferro, e davano del letame al campanile perchè crescesse.

[2] Quatre-vingt-dix-neuf moutons et un Champenois font cent bêtes.

Tenterden steeple 's the cause of the Goodwin Sands.

This proposition is commonly quoted as a flagrant example of bad logic, illustrating the fallacy of the reference *post hoc, ergo propter hoc.* A very quaint account of its origin is given in these words in one of Latimer's sermons : — " Mr. Moore was once sent with commission into Kent, to try out, if it might be, what was the cause of Goodwin's Sands, and the shelf which stopped up Sandwich Haven. Thither cometh Mr. Moore, and calleth all the country before him ; such as were thought to be men of experience, and men that could of likelihood best satisfy him of the matter concerning the stopping of Sandwich Haven. Among the rest came in before him an old man with a white head, and one that was thought to be little less than an hundred years old. When Mr. Moore saw this aged man he thought it expedient to hear him say his mind in this matter ; for, being so old a man, it was likely that he knew most in that presence, or company. So Mr. Moore called this old aged man unto him, and said, ' Father, tell me, if you can, what is the cause of the great arising of the sands and shelves here about this haven, which stop it up so that no ships can arrive here. You are the oldest man I can espy in all the company, so that if any man can tell the cause of it, you of all likelihood can say most to it, or at leastwise more than any man here assembled.' ' Yea, forsooth, good Mr. Moore,' quoth this old man, ' for I am well-nigh an hundred years old, and no man here in this company anything near my age.' ' Well, then,' quoth Mr. Moore, 'how say you to this matter? What think you to be the cause of these shelves and sands, which stop up Sandwich Haven?' 'Forsooth, sir,' quoth he, 'I am an old man; I think that Tenterton steeple is the cause of Goodwin's Sands. For I am an old man, sir,' quoth he; 'I may remember the building of Tenterton steeple, and I may remember when there was no steeple at all there. And before that Tenterton steeple was in building there was no manner of talking of any flats or sands that stopped up the haven; and therefore I think that Tenterton steeple is the cause of the decay and destroying of Sandwich Haven.'"

After all, this is not so palpable a *non sequitur* as it appears, for, says Fuller, "one story is good till another is told; and though this be all whereupon this proverb is generally grounded, I met since with a supplement thereunto: it is this. Time out of mind, money was constantly collected out of this county to fence the east banks thereof against the irruption of the sea, and such sums were deposited in the hands of the Bishop of Rochester; but because the sea had been quiet for many years without any encroaching, the bishop commuted this money to the building of a steeple and endowing a church at Tenterden. By this diversion of the collection for the maintenance of the banks, the sea afterwards broke in upon Goodwin Sands. And now the old man had told a rational tale, had he found but the due favor to finish it; and thus, sometimes, that is causelessly accounted ignorance of the speaker which is nothing but impatience in the auditors, unwilling to attend to the end of the discourse."

A loyal heart may be landed under Traitors' Bridge.

Every one who has passed down the Thames from London Bridge knows that archway in front of the Tower, under which boats conveying prisoners of state used to pass to Traitors' Stairs.

A knight of Cales, a gentleman of Wales, and a laird of the north countree;
A yeoman of Kent, with his yearly rent, will buy them out all three.

" Cales knights were made in that voyage by Robert, Earl of Essex, to the number of sixty, whereof (though many of great birth) some were of low fortunes; and therefore Queen Elizabeth was half offended with the earl for making knighthood so common.   Of the numerousness of Welsh gentlemen nothing need be said, the Welsh generally pretending to gentility.   Northern lairds are such who in Scotland hold lands in chief of the king, whereof some have no great revenue.   So that a Kentish yeoman (by the help of a hyperbole) may countervail," etc. — (*Fuller.*)   " A Spanish don, a German count, a French marquis, an Italian bishop, a Neapolitan cavalier, a Portuguese hidalgo, and a Hungarian noble make up a so-so company " (Italian).[1]

---

[1] Un don di Spagna, conte d'Allemagna, marchese di Francia, vescovo d'Italia, cavaglier di Napoli, idalgo di Portugullo, nobile d'Ungheria fanno una tal qual compagnia.

The Italians are wise before the fact, the Germans in the fact, the French after the fact. — *Italian.*[1]

The Italians are known by their singing, the French by their dancing, the Spaniards by their lording it, and the Germans by their drinking. — *Italian.*[2]

Where Germans are, Italians like not to be. — *Italian.*[3]

Italy, heads, holidays, and tempests. — *Italian.*[4]

A gentleman, who visited Dublin in the O'Connell times, gave it as the result of his experience there that Ireland was a land of groans, grievances, and invitations to dinner.

He that has to do with a Tuscan must not be blind. — *Italian.*[5]

There is a double meaning in the original. The same Italian word means Tuscan and poison.

It is better to be in the forest and eat pine cones than to live in a castle with Spaniards. — *Italian.*[6]

Because the frugal Spanish soldiers could subsist on diet on which men of other nations would starve. For them "Bread and radishes were a heavenly dinner" (Spanish).[7]

---

[1] Gl' Italiani saggi innanzi il fatto, i Tedeschi nel fatto, i Francesi dopo il fatto.

[2] L'Italiano al cantare, i Francesi al ballare, i Spagnuoli al bravare, i Tedeschi allo sbevacchiare, si conoscono.

[3] Dove stanno Tedesche, mal volontieri stanno Italiani.

[4] Italia, teste, feste, e tempeste.

[5] Chi ha da far con Tosco, non vuol esser losco.

[6] E meglio star al bosco, e mangiar pignuoli, che star in castello co' Spagnuoli.

[7] Pan y ravanillos, comer de Dios.

Abstract from a Spaniard all his good qualities, and there remains a Portuguese. — *Spanish.*

Every layman in Castile might make a king, every clerk a pope.
— *Spanish.*

If the overweening pride of the Spaniard appears in these two proverbs, the candor of the following must also be acknowledged —

Suckers of Spain, either late or never. — *Spanish.*[1]
Things of Spain. — *Spanish.*[2]

That is, abuses, anomalies, and faults of all kinds. See " Ford's Handbook," *passim.*

When the Spaniard sings, either he is mad or he has not a doit.
— *Spanish.*[3]

A Pole would rather steal a horse on Sunday than eat milk or butter on Friday. — *German.*[4]

Poland is the hell of peasants, the paradise of Jews, the purgatory of burghers, the heaven of nobles, and the gold mine of foreigners. — *German.*[5]

A Polish bridge, a Bohemian monk, a Swabian nun, Italian devotion, and German fasting are worth a bean. — *German.*[6]

If the devil came out of hell to fight there would forthwith be a Frenchman to accept the challenge. — *French.*[7]

---

[1] Socorros de España, ó tarde, ó nunca.

[2] Cosas de España.

[3] Quando el Español canta, ó rabia, ó no tiene blanca.

[4] Ein Pole würde eher am Sonntag ein Pferd stehlen, als am Freitag Milch oder Butter essen.

[5] Polen ist der Bauern Hölle, der Juden Paradies, der Bürger Fegefeuer, der Edelleute Himmel, und der Fremden Goldgrube.

[6] Eine Polnische Brücke, ein Böhmischer Mönkh eine Schabische Nonne, Welsche Andacht, und der Deutschen Fasten gelten eine Bohne.

[7] Si le diable sortait de l'enfer pour combattre, il se présenterait aussitôt un Français pour accepter le défi.

When the Frenchman sleeps the devil rocks him. — *French.*[1]

The Italians weep, the Germans screech, and the French sing.
— *French.*[2]

This is found word for word in Italian also, though it seems devised for the special glorification of Frenchmen. The Portuguese say —

The Frenchman sings well when his throat is moistened.
— *Portuguese.*[4]

The Germans have their wit in their fingers. — *French.*[4]

That means they are skilful workmen.

The emperor of Germany is the king of kings, the king of Spain king of men, the king of France king of asses, the king of England king of devils. — *French.*[5]

It is better to hear the lark sing than the mouse creep.

This was the proverb of the Douglases, adopted by every Border chief to express, as Sir Walter Scott observes, what the great Bruce had pointed out — that the woods and hills were the safest bulwarks of their country, instead of the fortified places which the English surpassed their neighbors in the art of assaulting or defending. The Servians have a similar saying:

---

[1] Quand le Français dort, le diable le berce.

[2] Les Italiens pleurent, les Allemands crient, et les Français chantent.

[3] Bein canta o Francez, papo molhado.

[4] Les Allemands ont l'esprit au doigts.

[5] L'empereur d'Allemagne est le roy des roys, le roy d'Espagne roy des hommes, le roy de France roy des asnes, et le roy d'Angleterre roy des diables.

"Better to look from the mountain than from the dungeon."

He that has missed seeing Seville has missed seeing a marvel.
— *Spanish.*[1]

See Naples and die. — *Italian.*[2]

There is but one Paris. — *French.*[3]

---

[1] Quien no ha vista Sevilla, no ha vista maraviglia.

[2] Vedi Napoli e poi mori.

[3] Il n'y a qu'un Paris.

INDEX.

Grass, 207
Greedy, 75
Grey mare, 21
Grindstone, 214
Gudewife, 73
Gudewilly, 111
Guest, 39

Habit, 93
Hackerton's cow, 108
Hair, 120, 141
Half, 151, 197
Halt, 147
Hameliness, 39
Hand, 169
Hand, in, 141
Handsaw, 153
Handsome, 9
Hang, 121, 124, 150, 179-181
Hanged, 81, 113, 121, 178, 180, 184
Hanging, 121, 123
Hangit, 105
Hangs, 158
Hanselled, 181
Hap, 51
Happy, 51, 183
Hardest step, 189
Hare, 98, 132
Hares, 141
Harried, 51
Harvest, 210,
Haste, 77
Hatter, 52
Hawk, 32
Hay, 134
Head, sound, 119
Hearsay, 159
Heart, 107, 127
Heaven, 132
Heaven, goes to, 183
Hell, 88, 89, 132, 198
Helmet, 61
Help, 43, 46, 156
Helps, 143,
Helped, 155
Hen, 21, 31
Hens, 112
Hen's egg, 83, 110
Herring, 102, 137
Hobby, 91
Hog, 32

Home, 34, 101
Homely, 34
Honest man, 128, 163
Honesty, 162
Honey, 33, 67, 78, 192, 210
Hood, 129
Hooly and fairly, 76
Hope, 121, 142, 143
Hopers, 88
Horn, 59, 130
Horse, 27, 47, 67, 82, 87, 111
Horse corn, 112
Horses, 98,
Horse, a good, 118
Horseman, 100
Host, 105, 137
Hostess, 8
Hound, 31
Hounds, 87, 98, 130, 146
House, 19, 35, 36, 78, 171
Hungarian, 218
Hunger, 185, 183, 205
Hungry, 78, 142, 186
Hunters, 128
Hurt, 54
Husbands, 20

Ibycus, 175
Idle, 68, 69
Ill, 52, 53, 55
Ill name, 158
Ill said, 121
Ill will, 158
Ill wind, 53
Intentions, 87, 88
Irishman, 212
Iron, 134
Italian, 218, 219, 221
Italianized Englishman, 213
Italy, 219

Jack, 50, 79
Janiveer, 207
January, 207
Jealousy, 11
Jedwood, 181
Jews, 220
Joan, 9
Jock Thief, 46
John Jelly, 102
Joyous heart, 86
Judgment, 155

5000232   INDEX.